HOW TO RAISE AND TRAIN A NEWFOUNDLAND

By Kitty Drury and Bill Linn

Distributed in the U.S.A. by T.F.H. Publications, Inc., 211 West Sylvania Avenue, P.O. Box 27, Neptune City, N.J. 07753; in England by T.F.H. (Gt. Britain) Ltd., 13 Nutley Lane, Reigate, Surrey; in Canada to the book store and library trade by Clarke, Irwin & Company, Clarwin House, 791 St. Clair Avenue West, Toronto 10, Ontario; in Canada to the pet trade by Rolf C. Hagen Ltd., 3225 Sartelon Street, Montreal 382, Quebec; in Southeast Asia by Y.W. Ong, 9 Lorong 36 Geylang, Singapore 14; in Australia and the south Pacific by Pet Imports Pty. Ltd., P.O. Box 149, Brookvale 2100, N.S.W., Australia. Published by T.F.H. Publications, Inc. Ltd., The British Crown Crown Colony of Hong Kong.

ACKNOWLEDGEMENTS

The authors, Mrs. Maynard K. Drury and Mr. Willis Linn, wish to thank all the members of the Newfoundland fancy who have generously contributed pictures, and the following who aided with editorial work and suggestions: Mrs. Virginia Barker, Mrs. Emma Halderman, Roger Richards, Miss Mary Drury, and the Reverend George Boardman.

Photos by Louise Van der Meid made with the co-operation of Mr. and Mrs. Robert Dibble, Mrs. Nancy Castro, Ruane Castro, and Bob Merriman.

ISBN 0-87666-341-2

Contents

1. DESCRIPTION, HISTORY, AND STANDARD 5
Description . . . The Newfoundland as a Companion . . . The Newfoundland as a Working Dog . . . The Newfoundland as a Lifesaver . . . Breed History . . . General Standard (As Interpreted by the Authors) . . . Official Standard as Approved by the American Kennel Club

2. BREED REQUIREMENTS 22
Exercise . . . Adult Food Requirements . . . Leads and Collars . . . Shelter Requirements . . . Climatic Limitations

3. GROOMING 25
Equipment . . . Methods of Grooming . . . Bathing

4. THE NEW PUPPY 28
Preparing for the Puppy's Arrival . . . Male or Female? . . . Where to Buy Your Puppy . . . Signs of Good Health . . . Age at Which Puppy Should Be Purchased . . . Papers . . . The Puppy's First Night With You . . . Your Puppy's Bed . . . Feeding Your Puppy . . . Transitional Diet . . . Breaking to Collar and Leash . . . Disciplining Your Puppy . . . Housebreaking . . . Outdoor Housebreaking

5. TRAINING 34
When to Start Training . . . Your Part in Training . . . The Training Voice . . . Training Lessons . . . Your Training Equipment and Its Use . . . Heeling . . . "Heel" Means "Sit," Too . . . Training To Sit . . . The "Lie Down" . . . The "Stay" . . . The "Come" on Command . . . Teaching to Come to Heel . . . The "Stand" . . . Training Schools and Classes . . . Advanced Training and Obedience Trials

6. BREEDING 42
The Question of Spaying . . . Sexual Physiology . . . Care of the Female in Estrus . . . Should You Breed Your Male? . . . Should You Breed Your Female? . . . When to Breed . . . How to Select a Stud . . . Preparation for Breeding . . . How Often Should You Breed Your Female? . . . The Importance and Application of Genetics

7. CARE OF THE MOTHER AND FAMILY 52
Prenatal Care of the Female . . . Preparation of Whelping Quarters . . . Supplies to Have on Hand . . . Whelping . . . Raising the Puppies . . . How to Take Care of a Large Litter . . . Caesarean Section
8. HEALTH 56
Watching Your Puppy's Health . . . The Useful Thermometer . . . First Aid . . . Importance of Inoculations . . . Distemper . . . Hepatitis . . . Leptospirosis . . . Rabies . . . Coughs, Colds, Bronchitis, Pneumonia . . . Internal Parasites . . . External Parasites . . . Skin Ailments . . . Eyes, Ears, Teeth, and Claws . . . Care of the Aged Dog
9. SHOWING 61
Types of Dog Shows . . . How to Enter . . . Advanced Preparation . . . The Day of the Show
BIBLIOGRAPHY 64

1. Description, History, and Standard

DESCRIPTION

The Newfoundland is a massive, strong, docile, gentle dog. Nothing is more fun than to be owned by one. As a guardian, companion, or working dog, he displays those qualities that make him loved the world over.

The Newfoundland's impressive size, intelligence, and gentle disposition make him an excellent guardian for children. He is particularly happy in this role, for it satisfies his unlimited capacity for devoted companionship. His size and amiability render him immune to the unintended roughness of small children. Babies tumble over and about him secure in the knowledge that no snap or growl will mar their play. When he becomes tired, he simply moves away, though his watchful eyes remain alert to their safety. Should danger threaten—a busy highway, a deep pool, a suspicious stranger—he is there, shielding his charges with his great strength, nudging them to safety. Gentle though he is, such is his size that few strangers would dare to challenge his devotion.

The Newfoundland, well known as one of the gentlest of all breeds, is an affectionate, understanding companion, as well as a brave and valiant rescuer of human life. Photo by Deo Paul.

Ch. Dryad's Beacon of Waseeka puts one in mind of "Nana," the faithful nursemaid in Sir James M. Barrie's classic tale for children, "Peter Pan."

That most famous of nursemaids, Nana, in *Peter Pan*, exemplified the true characteristics of her breed as she waited patiently through the long days for the Darling children to return. They complained, as all children do, that she was much too strict, and yet how happy they were to be back again under her loving care.

THE NEWFOUNDLAND AS A COMPANION

The Newfoundland as a companion requires little training. The rules regarding housebreaking and household behavior are easily learned and should be taught early. Insist quietly, but firmly, that he heel, sit, lie down, and stay on command, and you have laid the basis for behavior that will make him welcome everywhere.

The ancestors of the Newfoundland were carefully selected for their awareness of responsibility. Your dog displays this today in his desire to understand what is expected of him. His intense desire to please renders him sensitive to disapproval. Though puppies will be scamps, it is rare that discipline will require more than a stern command to insure willing obedience.

Do not tie up your Newfoundland or fence him in and abandon him for long periods. A run or pen is advisable for those times when he can not go with you. His search for companionship might well lead him across a busy highway or into a stranger's car. At other times keep him by your side, and he will develop his fullest potential as a devoted companion.

The Newfoundland's weather-resistant coat allows him to adapt easily to extremes of climate and temperature. Abrupt changes in temperature do not make him subject to colds or other respiratory ailments. He is equally happy lying quietly before the fire or buried deep in a snowdrift oblivious of blizzard winds.

THE NEWFOUNDLAND AS A WORKING DOG

The Newfoundland remains a working dog. The talents that he displays today are the same as those expected of him years ago. His ability in the water was highly developed by his original owners, the Indians and native fishermen of Newfoundland. Dogs were sent into the sea to pull heavy fishing nets back through the surf. The fish were loaded into carts and hauled into town. The dogs worked with a will in harness, hauling great weights with ease. It was estimated in the year 1815 that these dogs furnished the town of St. John's with labor valued at $4500-$5000 per day. A single dog would, by his labor, support his owner through the long winter.

During the 1800's, the Newfoundland pulled His Majesty's mail from one Newfoundland outpost to another, and for this service was honored by the issue of a stamp bearing his portrait. Later, when a new issue commemorated

The Newfoundland is still capable of assuming the draft duties he was originally bred for. Oquaga's Sea Diver II and Topsail's Black Velvet prove the Newfoundland combines beauty with utility. These dogs are owned and were trained by Mr. and Mrs. Hubert Garnsey, with whom they are pictured. Photo by Terence Gili.

the coronation of George VI, he was awarded the singular honor of being placed on the same stamp with the King.

Newfoundlands have also been used in sled teams. The explorer Elisha Kent Kane used his team of gray Newfoundlands in Greenland, not only to carry supplies but also to aid in rescuing members of the party who became lost. On the islands of St. Pierre and Miquelon, native teams pulled lumber from the woods to the sawmill.

Today, Newfoundlands pull carts for fun. They may be seen in exhibitions at specialty shows, in parades, on rural roads and urban streets, pulling children and adults alike. No miserable, dejected workers these! With tails wagging and heads up they carry delighted children into adventure in make-believe "stagecoaches" and "pirate ships." One need only see the shining eyes of a small crippled child who, when gently lifted into a cart, suddenly joins the pleasures of more fortunate playmates to realize that the money contributed to charities by such rides is only a small portion of the gift imparted.

THE NEWFOUNDLAND AS A LIFESAVER

The role of lifesaver is time-honored, and it is here that the Newfoundland excels. His remarkable ability in the water and his concern for the people around him have combined to save many lives. All hope for those aboard the ship *Ethie* had been abandoned as she tossed on storm-lashed reefs, until

Many Newfoundland owners perpetuate the breed's proud record as a lifesaver. Here Mr. and Mrs. Maynard Drury are shown in a typical training session with Ch. Dryad's Pilot and Ch. Dryad's Lighthouse Beam.

Ch. Montana Mustang Arno, owned by Mrs. James C. Dudley. This is an example of a fine Landseer Newfoundland. Arno is believed to be the only Landseer ever to have won best of breed at the Westminster Kennel Club. He is also the winner of the national specialty. Photo by Evelyn Shafer.

the ship's dog fought his way through breaking surf with a line gripped tightly in his mouth. A boatswain's chair was attached and all hands were saved. Napoleon owed his life to a Newfoundland who pulled him from the water when he, unable to swim, fell overboard in the darkness on his way to Elba.

Today our dogs remain alert to swimmers in distress and instinctively swim to the rescue when help is needed. Many a mother has blessed the dog who has faithfully guarded her small children as they played in the water. Simple training sends them swimming to recover the drifting boat, the dropped paddle, or the wayward fishing pole.

Those who recall that the Newfoundland and the Labrador Retriever descend from a common ancestor will not be surprised that the breed is also a fine hunting dog. He has what is known to hunters as a soft mouth, trains easily, and is a fine retriever. Icy waters do not deter him, and he does his work well.

At times his devotion to duty exceeds even that most powerful of instincts: self-preservation. During the siege of Hong Kong in World War II, the mascot of the Royal Winnipeg Grenadiers seized an enemy grenade and plunged out of the circle of men into whose midst it had fallen. The grenade exploded, and sorrowing friends praised his bravery and intelligence.

BREED HISTORY

The Newfoundland is one of the few breeds indigenous to the North American continent. Whether his forbears were the big black Bear Dogs of Norway left here by Leif Ericson (A.D. 1000) or descendants of Tibetan Mastiffs that crossed over from the Asian continent is still a matter of controversy. We do know that early explorers in the seventeenth century found large Mastiff-like dogs on the island of Newfoundland. The first mention of the Newfoundland as a distinct breed comes from the journal of Sir Joseph Banks, who in 1700 wrote that "a man from Trepassy had a breed he called 'the Newfoundland Dog'."

The breed was later exported to England, where it became very popular. It is presumed that the Mastiff-like dogs were crossed with the English Mastiff to obtain the size and massiveness which are common to the breed today. It is possible that a cross was made with the white Pyrenees Dog of the Basque fishermen. An early cross with the Springer Spaniel may account for the black and white coloration of the Landseer Newfoundland. The name Landseer was derived from that of the artist Sir Edwin Landseer, who greatly popularized the breed with his many paintings of the black and white variety.

Specimens of the breed were owned by the English Royal Family during this era. A Newfoundland who saved the life of his master lies buried in the grounds of Windsor Castle.

In the United States, the first reference to the breed was in 1639. It stated that a "large, black, wooly dog" was used as an article of trade with the

This lovely Newfoundland puppy seems to reflect on his proud heritage and his royal ownership. He, along with two others, is owned by King Hassan II of Morocco. The three puppies were bred by the Little Bear Kennels.

Indians during the bargaining for Gardiner's Island, N.Y. In Revolutionary times, Samuel Adams owned a Newfoundland called "Que Que," who was known to have harassed the Redcoats. From that time on, the breed gradually gained in popularity until in the late 1880's the family life of a country home was not considered complete without a Newfoundland. The dogs were so loved that they were depicted on all sorts of objects. Today the Newfoundland fancier prizes these antique statues, stamps, pins, buttons, pictures, toy banks, and articles of needlework.

The trend toward large or small breeds in the popular fancy varies with the times. Terriers, spaniels, and toy dogs were the fashion for many years. The big breeds are again coming into their own, and the Newfoundland is enjoying a "new day." The average number of Newfoundlands registered with the American Kennel Club during the 1930's was 106, during the 1940's, 190. In the past year, registrations climbed to a new high of 361. This gradual increase in breed numbers is an indication that breeders have succeeded in their aim to maintain those qualities always associated with the breed: disposition, soundness, and intelligence. Quality has never been sacrificed for quantity.

Canadian Ch. Romy v.d. Schurz, owned by Harbour Beem Kennels. Sire: Int. Ch. Bob v.d. Warte; dam: Helga v.d. Schurz. This dog is a Swiss import.

The Newfoundland is a canine gentleman who thoroughly enjoys life. Black Enchantress and Ch. Irwindyl's Minstrel Man get ready to take a spin with their owners, Mr. and Mrs. Charles Finter. Photo by Stewart.

Today there are about ten or fifteen Newfoundland kennels in the United States. Many more puppies are bred by owners of a single bitch who take pride in breeding once a year to a good stud. The resulting puppies are raised with an abundance of loving care. Most responsible breeders feel that disposition and soundness are so fundamental that they guarantee their puppies for disposition and freedom from congenital defects up to the age of one year, with the option of replacing any puppy that does not live up to standard.

In the early 1950's a committee appointed by the Newfoundland Club of America studied the pedigrees of all champions of record of the previous 20 years. It was found that every champion could trace its ancestry to one of the following three English imports: Ch. Baron, Ch. Shelton Cabin Boy, and Ch. Harlingen Neptune of Waseeka. All three dogs were sired by the English Champion Siki.

Newfoundlands today are being bred not only in the United States and Canada but also in England, Switzerland, Germany, Holland, Thailand, Sweden, Norway, Ireland, and Australia. Others have been exported to other countries and will undoubtedly be bred in the future.

GENERAL STANDARD (As Interpreted by the Authors)

The breed standard is a criterion, or set of regulations, that determines the manifestation of breed characteristics. It is a description of the breed in technical terms, used as a guide by breeders for the evaluation and selection of puppies and adult dogs and by judges for the selection of winning dogs.

The original standard was drawn up and formally adopted in 1879. The present standard differs only slightly from the original and consists of four sections: general conformation, head, body, and movement.

GENERAL CONFORMATION

PURPOSE

The Newfoundland is a working dog. In order to fulfill his purpose as a water retriever and draft animal, he must be large, strong, sound, have webbed feet, and a heavy, water-resistant coat. As a guardian of children he must possess a gentle disposition, as evidenced by his benevolent expression and docile action. He is never shy or timid.

GENERAL APPEARANCE

The Newfoundland is square in body (proportionate length and height) and gains his height from depth of chest, not length of leg.

Ch. Sarja's Sir Lionel of Irwindyl, owned by Mrs. Arthur Irwin. Tauskey Photo.

Many owners enjoy their Newfoundlands in the show ring as well as in the home. In addition to being a pleasant companion, your Newfoundland may make you the proud owner of a winning dog. Photo by Louise Van der Meid.

COLOR

Most Newfoundlands are black or black and white in combination (Landseers). Many otherwise solid black dogs have white spots on their chests, white toes, and white-tipped tails. Landseers should have black heads with a white blaze, black saddle, and black symmetrical markings on legs and tail. Brown, gray, bronze, and black dogs with gray or brown markings on toes and chest are comparatively rare and are similar to blacks in all other respects. When appearing in show competition, all colors are judged according to the same standard.

SIZE

Size is to be encouraged as long as symmetry and balance are maintained. Smallness is discouraged as uncharacteristic of the breed. The average adult male should stand a minimum of 28 inches high at the withers, adult females, 26 inches. Average weights at maturity approximate 150 pounds in the male, 120 pounds in the female.

Ch. Little Bear's Sailing Free, owned by Mrs. William Kurth. Sire: Ch. Little Bear's Canicula Campio; Little Bear's Mia Maija. This dog is shown winning first in the working ground at the Greater Lowell Kennel Club after winning best of breed at the Newfoundland Club of America Specialty show. This fine win was scored under judge Reginald M. Cleveland. The dog was handled here by Charley Meyer.

The Newfoundland standard states that the male Newfoundland should always be slightly larger than the female. This pair (male left and female right) clearly illustrate this specification. Both should give the impression of imposing strength and power regardless of sex. Photo by Louise Van der Meid.

COAT

The Newfoundland has a long, full, double coat which contributes to the impression of great size. The coat is of a coarse nature and resists water. The undercoat is soft and wooly and affords protection from the cold. The coat insulates against extremes of temperature in summer heat, as well as winter cold.

HEAD

The head of the Newfoundland is given major consideration, for it conveys that expression of benevolent dignity so characteristic of the breed. The eyes should be dark brown, set well apart, and showing no haw or redness. The skull should be broad and rounded, the muzzle deep. No wrinkles should appear on the face. In comparison with the head of the St. Bernard, the Newfoundland head does not have well-defined stop, and the nose is rounded, rather than square. The ears are triangular in shape and lie close to the head. They are never long or pricked. The teeth should be set in either a level or scissors bite.

BODY

The body of the Newfoundland shows a broad muscular neck well set onto

Canadian and American Ch. Captain Morgan's Prince, owned by Mr. and Mrs. Fred Kearsey. Sire: Ch. Topsail's Captain Henry; dam: Deneault's Queen. This typical head study well illustrates the expression of patient dignity and deep sagacity associated with the Newfoundland.

Ch. Caldwell's Yulie's Top Sail, owned by James L. McMahon. Sire: Ch. Irwindyl's Yule Log; dam: Ch. Irwindyl's Lady Loralee. The typical Newfoundland should always impress the observer as a dog of unlimited strength and endurance. The message should be conveyed even in a show pose that a Newfoundland could carry a lost voyager to safety in heavy seas as easily as he can win a best of breed.

the shoulders. The chest should be broad, reaching just below the elbow as viewed from the side. Body length, as measured from sternum to point of tail, should roughly equal the distance from the shoulder (withers) to the ground. The back is broad, strong, and straight, contributing to the square appearance. Rear and front legs should be straight and well muscled. The tail should be long, reaching to the hock. It should be straight, carried with a slight curve when the dog is in motion, but never curled over the back.

MOVEMENT

Movement, or gait, is given great emphasis. Symmetry and balance may be apparent in the standing dog, but will disappear as he moves unless he is structurally sound. The dog should move with freedom and ease, legs moving in straight lines when viewed from the front and rear. A characteristic roll will be evident at the trot.

The above description describes in brief the perfect Newfoundland and the aim of breeders. Many dogs possess minor faults but make ideal pets because they have the true Newfoundland disposition. You may never find the dog that ideally expresses the Standard in all respects, but we trust that you will experience the faithful devotion and sweet companionship that are yours when you are owned by a Newfoundland.

OFFICIAL STANDARD AS APPROVED BY THE AMERICAN KENNEL CLUB

SYMMETRY AND GENERAL APPEARANCE—The dog should impress the eye with strength and great activity. He should move freely on his legs with the body swung loosely between them, so that a slight roll in gait should not be objectionable; but at the same time, a weak or hollow back, slackness of the loins or cow hocks, should be a decided fault.

HEAD—Should be broad and massive, the occipital bone well developed, there should be no decided stop, and the muzzle should be short, clean cut, and rather square in shape, and covered with short, fine hair.

COAT—Should be flat and dense, of a coarsish texture and oily nature, and capable of resisting the water. If brushed the wrong way, it should fall back into its place naturally.

BODY—Should be well ribbed up with a broad back. A neck, strong, well set on the shoulders and back, with strong muscular loins.

FORELEGS—Should be perfectly straight, well covered with muscle, elbows in but well let down and feathered all down.

HINDQUARTERS AND LEGS—Should be very strong, the legs should have great freedom of action, and a little feather. Slackness of loins and cow hocks are a great defect; dewclaws are objectionable and should be removed.

CHEST—Should be deep and fairly broad and well covered with hair, but not to such an extent as to form a frill.

BONE—Massive throughout, but not to give a heavy, inactive appearance.

FEET—Should be large and well shaped. Splayed or turned-out are objectionable.

TAIL—Should be of moderate length, reaching down a little below the hocks, it should be of fair thickness, and well covered with long hair, but not to form a flag. When the dog is standing still and not excited, it should hang downward with a slight curve at the end; but when the dog is in motion, it should be carried a trifle up, and when he is excited, straight out, with a slight curve at the end. Tails with a kink in them, or curled over the back, are very objectionable.

EARS—Should be small, set well back, square with the skull, lie close to the head, and covered with short hair and no fringe.

EYES—Should be small, of a dark color, rather deeply set but not showing any haw, and they should be rather widely apart.

Ch. Dryad's Brown Betty, owned by Seaward Kennels and shown here with her handler, Mrs. Edwin Cummings. Betty is the only brown champion in the history of the Newfoundland breed. Photo by Evelyn Shafer.

COLOR—Dull, jet black. A slight tinge of bronze or a splash of white on chest and toes is not objectionable.

HEIGHT AND WEIGHT—Size and weight are very desirable so long as symmetry is maintained. A fair average height at the shoulders is 28 in. for a dog and 26 in. for a bitch, and a fair average weight is, respectively: dogs, 140 to 150 lbs.; bitches, 110 to 120 lbs.

OTHER THAN BLACK—Should in all respects follow the black except in color, which may be almost any, so long as it disqualifies for the black class, but the colors most to be encouraged are white and black or bronze. Beauty in markings to be taken greatly into consideration.

Black dogs that have only white toes and white breasts and white tip to tail should be exhibited in the classes provided for "black."

2. Breed Requirements

EXERCISE

Your Newfoundland puppy will maintain a level of activity consistent with his body requirements for growth and exercise. As an adult, he may gradually content himself with comfortable observations of the family (his life) from a cool spot on the lawn. Among a family of active children, the grown dog may stay in good physical condition by active play, retrieving, pulling sleds and carts, and accompanying the children on all those expeditions to which children are prone.

Prime physical condition is essential if the dog is to be shown or bred. Slow daily conditioning by an hour's run, a mile or two at a hard trot, or a long swim will harden muscles and give him a driving, powerful gait. The unconditioned, soft-muscled dog appears loose-jointed and wobbly by comparison.

Canadian Ch. Eskimo's Grey Mug, owned by Mrs. Veronica Payne. This typical dog is shown winning best of breed at the Newfoundland Club of America Specialty under judge K. Drury, held with the Trenton Kennel Club in May of 1960. Photo by William Brown.

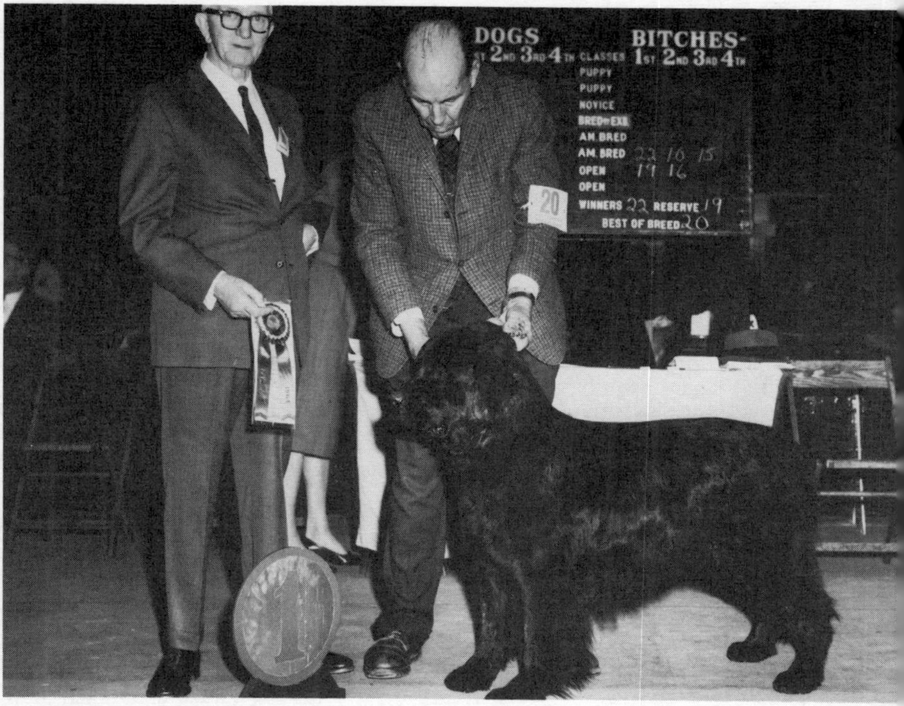

Ch. Little Bear's Thunder, U.D., owned by Roger E. Richards and bred by Little Bear Kennels. Sire: Ch. Little Bear's Canicula Campio; dam: Little Bear's Indian Teaberry. Thunder is shown winning best of breed at the Westminster Kennel Club under judge William Ackland and is handled by E. J. Carver. Photo by Evelyn Shafer.

The bitch in whelp who is exercised regularly will maintain appetite and muscle tone, and whelp more easily.

ADULT FOOD REQUIREMENTS

There are almost as many feeding methods as there are foods to be fed. A grown dog, strictly speaking, can live on almost any food. For maximum development of structural potential, certain substances are needed; table scraps alone cannot provide a balanced diet.

An average diet for an adult Newfoundland (two to seven years of age) would consist of 1½ pounds of a good commercial kibble or dry meal combined with enough warm water, milk, or beef broth to moisten, plus 1 to 1½ pounds of raw or seared meat, all mixed to the consistency of cornbeef hash. If the meat is very lean, ½ pound of suet should be added.

Some breeders now feed cafeteria style, leaving a good commercial dry kibble available to the dogs at all times and supplementing with dried milk and corn oil.

Optimum weights vary from dog to dog. If your dog maintains a healthy, glossy coat, bright eyes, and a good, but not oversoft, covering of flesh over the ribs and backbone, you are probably feeding him properly.

An adequate supply of fresh water must be available at all times.

LEADS AND COLLARS

It is often convenient to have two leads of different lengths. Purchase a six-foot webbed or leather lead for training, and for those long walks where there are few obstacles. For training purposes, especially during the "stay" exercises, the length allows you to move a greater distance while maintaining control over your dog. During walks he may roam farther afield and thus exercise more freely.

A second leather lead, 2½ to 3 feet long, is useful in town, where he is to remain at heel, or while you are showing him.

Purchase a collar for your puppy and put it on him early so that he will become accustomed to it. Check it for size often, as his growth will astound even you, his owner. When he is about seven months old, buy a good, heavily plated, non-beveled chain training collar. Contrary to popular opinion, the chain collar is neither dangerous nor cruel when properly used.

Put the dog at your left side and place the collar around his neck so that the free end, to which the lead is attached, runs across the top of his neck toward you. In this position, the collar will tighten only when pressure is applied by the leash, and will release immediately. The puppy soon learns that dragging or lunging ahead tightens the collar, whereas walking quietly at your side causes it to hang loosely and comfortably around his neck.

Begin lead training early; eight weeks of age is not too soon. Make each step gradual; associate the lead with pleasant excursions. Use patience and lavish praise, and your puppy will soon respond by walking gaily and obediently at your side.

SHELTER REQUIREMENTS

Many Newfoundlands sleep in their owners' homes. Many more prefer to live outdoors winter and summer. Decide when you bring the puppy home where you wish him to sleep, and he will soon identify with it.

If your dog is to sleep outdoors, his house should be large enough to accommodate his bulk (some 130 or more pounds stretched out 6 feet), off the ground, and free of drafts. In winter, cedar shavings or hay will serve to further insulate the kennel floor. Cedar shavings have the added advantage of not harboring skin parasites.

In summer, adequate shade must be provided.

CLIMATIC LIMITATIONS

The Newfoundland has proven adaptable to a wide range of climatic conditions. While he may be at his best in the colder regions which resemble his ancestral Newfoundland, he does adjust well to the southern and southwestern states. A dog raised in a warmer climate adjusts more easily to subtropical conditions than a dog raised in northern climes.

3. Grooming

The grooming of your dog not only makes him look nice but also cleans his coat and skin, thus doing away with dirt, mats, and loose undercoat which often cause skin trouble and eczema. These conditions are difficult to clear up, as well as being expensive to treat. Newfoundlands love the attention they receive while being groomed. If you do it regularly, it is much easier, as you will not have to use a stripper on mats and not have a tug-of-war with snarls, which hurts the dog and takes away from the pleasure and companionship usually afforded.

EQUIPMENT

Your local petshop will have a dazzling array of grooming tools from which you may choose. We suggest the following basic tools:

1—all metal, chrome-plated, 6″-long, coarse-spaced comb

1—wooden-handled English rake comb (for removing burrs)

1—heavy-bristled large oval brush, furnished with a leather loop handle.

These basic tools are not expensive, and your experience will soon tell you that perhaps you prefer a finer tooth comb or some other tool your dealer offers, which will suit you and your dog better.

Remember: make it a habit to groom your dog often. He will look better, feel better, and love you more.

METHODS OF GROOMING

Your Newfoundland's coat will have a slight oily feeling unless he has just been bathed. It will lie flat against his body, and, since he has two coats, it will take some practice to groom your dog quickly and thoroughly. Don't waste your time by combing with the lay of the coat—do it backwards. Start at the bottom rear of the body coat and work towards the head. If you are right handed, lift the coat with the left hand until the skin is visible and comb from the skin out—getting all the inner coat as well as the outer. Do the dog's topline, then the sides and tail, in this manner. Make him lie down and do his stomach and legs. Now take your oval brush and brush him thoroughly with long, smooth strokes in the direction his hair lies naturally. His coat will shine, and with the exception of trimming, your Newfoundland should be ready for the show ring.

Even if you are not going to show your dog, an occasional trimming is in order. It is quite simple.

Feet: In trimming the Newfoundland's feet, clean the dead hair out from between the toes by pulling the hair upward and using trimming scissors to thin it. Cut away the excess hair around the pads. On the forelegs, trim away the feather from the base of the paw up the back of the legs to the heel button. On the rear legs, trim the feather off about one inch above the back of the paws.

Ears: If the ears look shaggy, trim away the excess with thinning scissors. Do not use a straight scissors, as this will give too much of a cut appearance.

Whiskers: Use a blunt-nosed pair of scissors to cut off the whiskers around the muzzle and over the eyes. This work tickles your dog, and you will soon see the reason for using blunt-nosed scissors.

Claws: An active dog rarely needs his claws trimmed. Claws are naturally worn down when the dog walks on stones and other hard surfaces. Check his claws—if they seem too long, clip off the dead portion with a claw clipper. Be careful not to cut the quick. The claws should just touch the floor when the dog stands naturally.

There is a wide variety of grooming tools which can be used on the Newfoundland with good results. Many owners prefer a wire slicker, such as the one shown here. Photo by Louise Van der Meid.

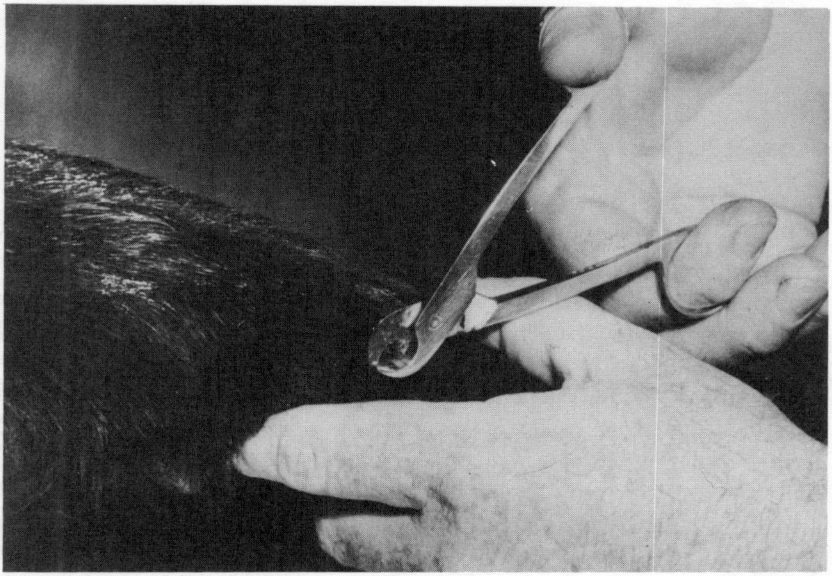

The Newfoundland's claws should be checked periodically and trimmed down if they are too long. Care should be taken so that the quick is not severed in the process. Photo by Louise Van der Meid.

Cleaning Ears: Nothing smaller than your finger should be used to clean inside a Newfoundland's ear. Dip cotton in rubbing alcohol and then gently wipe out the ear. It should be done as often as the ears appear dirty or smelly.

BATHING

Your Newfoundland will be kept fairly clean simply by brushing, but several times a year you may wish to bathe him. After you have brushed your dog well, he should be placed in a suitable large tub, or, if you have the choice, it is much preferable to take him outside on the lawn and wet him down thoroughly with the garden hose. Apply a good commercial dog shampoo (never a detergent), and work it into his coat with a large scrubbing brush. Dip the scrubbing brush into a pail of warm water from time to time; this helps to work up a lather. Rinse off the suds with the hose and follow with a pail of warm water as a final rinse. If you live near a body of water where your dog is accustomed to swim, put on your bathing suit and follow the same procedure as above, using lake water instead of the hose. To rinse, go right out in the water with him and have him swim around while you help with the rinse by stroking his coat the wrong way under water.

Don't worry about your Newfoundland catching cold. Remember that he often takes a dip, even in the middle of winter.

If you are going to show your dog, bathe him a week before the show so that his natural oil will return to give his coat its usual shine.

4. The New Puppy

PREPARING FOR THE PUPPY'S ARRIVAL

Because at least three out of four prospective purchasers of dogs want to buy a young rather than an adult or almost adult dog, the problem of preparing for the arrival of a permanent canine house guest almost always means preparing for the arrival of a puppy. This is not to say that there is anything wrong with purchasing an adult dog; on the contrary, such a purchase has definite advantages in that it often allows freedom from housebreaking chores and rigorous feeding schedules, and these are of definite benefit to prospective purchasers who have little time to spare. Since the great majority of dog buyers, however, prefer to watch their pet grow from sprawlingly playful puppyhood to dignified maturity, buying a dog, practically speaking, means buying a puppy.

Before you get a puppy be sure that you are willing to take the responsibility of training him and caring for his physical needs. His early training is most important, as an adult dog that is a well-behaved member of the family is the end product of your early training. Remember that your new puppy knows only a life of romping with his littermates and the security of being with his mother, and that coming into your home is a new and sometimes frightening experience for him. He will adjust quickly if you are patient with him and show him what you expect of him. If there are small children in the family be sure that they do not abuse him or play roughly with him. A puppy plays hard, but he also requires frequent periods of rest. Before he comes, decide where he is to sleep and where he is to eat. If your puppy does not have a collar, find out the size he requires and buy an inexpensive one, as he will soon outgrow it. Have the proper grooming equipment on hand. Consult the person from whom you bought the puppy as to the proper food for your puppy, and learn the feeding time and amount that he eats a day. Buy him some toys—usually the breeder will give you some particular toy or toys which he has cherished as a puppy to add to his new ones and to make him less homesick. Get everything you need from your petshop *before* you bring the puppy home.

MALE OR FEMALE?

Before buying your puppy you should have made a decision as to whether you want a male or a female. Unless you want to breed your pet and raise a litter of puppies, your preference as to the sex of your puppy is strictly a personal choice. Both sexes are pretty much the same in disposition and character, and both make equally good pets.

WHERE TO BUY YOUR PUPPY

Although petshop owners are necessarily restricted from carrying all breeds in stock, they know the best dog breeders and are sometimes able to supply quality puppies on demand. In cases in which a petshop owner is unable to obtain a dog for you, he can still refer you to a good source, such as a reputable kennel. If your local petshop proprietor is unable to either obtain a dog for you or refer you to someone from whom you can purchase one, don't give up: there are other avenues to explore. The American Kennel Club will furnish you addresses. Additional sources of information are the various magazines devoted to the dog fancy.

SIGNS OF GOOD HEALTH

Picking out a healthy, attractive little fellow to join the family circle is a different matter from picking a show dog; it is also a great deal less complicated. Often the puppy will pick you. If he does, and it is mutual admiration at first sight, he is the best puppy for you. At a reliable kennel or petshop the owner will be glad to answer your questions and to point out the difference between pet and show-quality puppies. Trust your eyes and hands to tell if the puppies are sound in body and temperament. Ears and eyes should not have suspicious discharges. Legs should have strong bones; bodies should have solid muscles. Coats should be clean. Lift the hair to see if the skin is free of scales and parasites.

Temperament can vary from puppy to puppy in the same litter. There is always one puppy which will impress you by his energy and personality. He loves to show off and will fling himself all over you and his littermates, and everyone who comes to see the puppies falls in love with him. However, do not overlook the more reserved puppy. Most dogs are wary of strangers, so reserve may indicate caution, not a timid puppy. He may calmly accept your presence when he senses that all is well. Such a puppy should be a steady reliable dog when mature. In any event, never force yourself on a puppy — let him come to you. Reliable breeders and petshops will urge you to take your puppy to the veterinarian of your choice to have the puppy's health checked, and will allow you at least two days in which to have it done. It should be clearly understood whether rejection by a veterinarian for health reasons means that you have the choice of another puppy from that litter or that you get your money back.

AGE AT WHICH PUPPY SHOULD BE PURCHASED

A puppy should be at least six weeks of age before you take him home. Many breeders will not let puppies go before they are two months old. In general, the puppy you buy for show and breeding should be five or six months old. If you want a show dog, remember that not even an expert can predict with 100% accuracy what a small puppy will be when he grows up.

PAPERS

When you buy a purebred dog you should receive his American Kennel Club registration certificate (or an application form to fill out), a pedigree, and a health certificate made out by the breeder's veterinarian. The registration certificate is the official A.K.C. paper. If the puppy was named and registered by his breeder you will want to complete the transfer and send it, with the fee, to the American Kennel Club. They will transfer the dog to your ownership in their records and send a new certificate to you. If you receive, instead, an application for registration, you should fill it out, choosing a name for your dog, and mail it, with the fee, to the A.K.C.

The pedigree is a chart showing your puppy's ancestry and is not a part of his official papers. The health certificate will tell what shots have been given and when the next ones are due. Your veterinarian will be appreciative of this information, and will continue with the same series of shots if they have not been completed. The health certificate will also give the dates on which the puppy has been wormed. Ask your veterinarian whether rabies shots are required in your locality. Most breeders will give you food for a few days along with instructions for feeding so that your puppy will have the same diet he is accustomed to until you can buy a supply at your petshop.

THE PUPPY'S FIRST NIGHT WITH YOU

The puppy's first night at home is likely to be disturbing to the family. Keep in mind that suddenly being away from his mother, brothers, and sisters is a new experience for him; he may be confused and frightened. If you have a special room in which you have his bed, be sure that there is nothing there with which he can harm himself. Be sure that all lamp cords are out of his reach and that there is nothing that he can tip or pull over. Check furniture that he might get stuck under or behind and objects that he might chew. If you want him to sleep in your room he probably will be quiet all night, reassured by your presence. If left in a room by himself he will cry and howl, and you will have to steel yourself to be impervious to his whining. After a few nights alone he will adjust. The first night that he is alone it is wise to put a loud-ticking alarm clock, as well as his toys, in the room with him. The alarm clock will make a comforting noise, and he will not feel that he is alone.

YOUR PUPPY'S BED

Every dog likes to have a place that is his alone. He holds nothing more sacred than his own bed whether it be a rug, dog crate, or dog bed. If you get your puppy a bed be sure to get one which discourages chewing. Also be sure that the bed is large enough to be comfortable for him when he is fully grown. Locate it away from drafts and radiators. A word might be said here in defense of the crate, which many pet owners think is cruel and confining. Given a choice, a young dog instinctively selects a secure place

Special dog feeding and watering utensils are so designed as to safeguard your pet from dangerous porcelain chips. These utensils are easy to keep clean, too.

in which to lounge, rest, or sleep. The walls and ceiling of a crate, even a wire one, answer that need. Once he regards his crate as a safe and reassuring place to stay, you will be able to leave him alone in the house.

FEEDING YOUR PUPPY

As a general rule, a puppy from weaning time (six weeks) to three months of age should have *four meals a day;* from three months to six months, *three meals;* from six months to one year, *two meals*. After a year, a dog does well on *one meal daily*. There are as many feeding schedules as there are breeders, and puppies do fine on all of them, so it is best for the new owner to follow the one given him by the breeder of his puppy. Remember that all dogs are individuals. The amount that will keep your dog in good health is right for him, not the "rule-book" amount. A feeding schedule to give you some idea of what the average puppy will eat is as follows:

Morning meal:	Puppy meal with milk.
Afternoon meal:	Meat mixed with puppy meal, plus a vitamin-mineral supplement.
Evening meal:	Same as afternoon meal, but without a vitamin-mineral supplement.

Do not change the amounts in your puppy's diet too rapidly. If he gets diarrhea it may be that he is eating too much, so cut back on his food and when he is normal again increase his food more slowly.

There is a canned food made especially for puppies which you can buy only by a veterinarian's prescription. Some breeders use this very successfully from weaning to three months.

TRANSITIONAL DIET

Changing over to an adult program of feeding is not difficult. Very often the puppy will change himself; that is, he will refuse to eat some of his meals. He adjusts to his one meal (or two meals) a day without any trouble at all.

BREAKING TO COLLAR AND LEASH

Puppies are usually broken to a collar before you bring them home, but even if yours has never worn one it is a simple matter to get him used to it. Put a loose collar on him for a few hours at a time. At first he may scratch at it and try to get it off, but gradually he will take it as a matter of course. To break him to a lead, attach his leash to his collar and let him drag it around. When he becomes used to it pick it up and gently pull him in the direction you want him to go. He will think it is a game, and with a bit of patience on your part he will allow himself to be led.

DISCIPLINING YOUR PUPPY

The way to have a well-mannered adult dog is to give him firm basic training while he is a puppy. When you say "*No*" you must mean "*No*." Your dog will respect you only if you are firm. A six- to eight-weeks-old puppy is old enough to understand what "*No*" means. The first time you see your puppy doing something he shouldn't be doing, chewing something he shouldn't chew, or wandering in a forbidden area, it's time to teach him. Shout, "*No*." Puppies do not like loud noises, and your misbehaving pet will readily connect the word with something unpleasant. Usually a firm "*No*" in a disapproving tone of voice is enough to correct your dog, but occasionally you get a puppy that requires a firmer hand, especially as he grows older. In this case hold your puppy firmly and slap him gently across the hindquarters. If this seems cruel, you should realize that no dog resents being disciplined if he is caught in the act of doing something wrong, and your puppy will be intelligent enough to know what the slap was for.

After you have slapped him and you can see that he has learned his lesson, call him to you and talk to him in a pleasant tone of voice — praise him for coming to you. This sounds contradictory, but it works with a puppy. He immediately forgives you, practically tells you that it was his fault and that he deserved his punishment, and promises that it will not happen again. This form of discipline works best and may be used for all misbehaviors.

Never punish your puppy by chasing him around, making occasional swipes with a rolled-up newspaper; punish him only when you have a firm hold on him. Above all, never punish your dog after having called him to you. He must learn to associate coming to you with something pleasant.

HOUSEBREAKING

While housebreaking your puppy do not let him have the run of the house. If you do you will find that he will pick out his own bathroom, which may be in your bedroom or in the middle of the living room rug. Keep him confined to a small area where you can watch him, and you will be able to train him much more easily and speedily. A puppy does not want to dirty his bed, but he does need to be taught where he should go. Spread papers over his living quarters, then watch him carefully. When you notice him starting to whimper, sniff the floor, or run agitatedly in little circles, rush him to the place that you want to serve as his relief area and gently hold him there until he relieves himself. Then praise him lavishly. When you remove the soiled papers, leave a small damp piece so that the puppy's sense of smell will lead him back there next time. If he makes a mistake, wash the area at once with warm water, followed by a rinse with water and vinegar or sudsy ammonia. This will kill the odor and prevent discoloration. It shouldn't take more than a few days for him to get the idea of using newspapers. When he becomes fairly consistent, reduce the area of paper to a few sheets in a corner. As soon as you think he has the idea fixed in his mind, you can let him roam around the house a bit, but keep an eye on him. It might be best to keep him on leash the first few days so that you can rush him back to his paper at any signs of an approaching accident.

The normal healthy puppy will want to relieve himself when he wakes up in the morning, after each feeding, and after strenuous exercise. During early puppyhood any excitement, such as the return home of a member of the family or the approach of a visitor, may result in floor-wetting, but that phase should pass in a few weeks. Keep in mind that you can't expect too much from your puppy until he is about five months old. Before that, his muscles and digestive system just aren't under his control.

OUTDOOR HOUSEBREAKING

You can begin outdoor training on leash even while you are paper-training your puppy. First thing in the morning take him outdoors (to the curb, if you are in the city) and walk him back and forth in a small area until he relieves himself. He will probably make a puddle and then walk around, uncertain of what is expected of him. You can try standing him over a newspaper, which may give him the idea. Some dog trainers use glycerine suppositories at this point for fast action. Praise your dog every time taking him outside brings results, and he will get the idea. You'll find, when you begin the outdoor training, that the male puppy usually requires a longer walk than the female. Both male and female puppies will squat. It isn't until he is older that the male dog will begin to lift his leg. If you hate to give up your sleep, you can train your puppy to go outdoors during the day and use the paper at night.

5. Training

WHEN TO START TRAINING

You should never begin SERIOUS obedience training before your dog is seven or eight months old. (Some animal psychologists state that puppies can begin training when seven weeks old, if certain techniques are followed. These techniques, however, are still experimental and should be left to the professional trainer to prove their worth.) While your dog is still in his early puppyhood, concentrate on winning his confidence so he will love and admire you. This will make his training easier, since he will do anything to please you. Basic training can be started at the age of three or four months. He should be taught to walk nicely on a leash, sit and lie down on command, and come when he is called.

YOUR PART IN TRAINING

You must patiently demonstrate to your dog what each word of command means. Guide him with your hands and the training leash, reassuring him with your voice, through whatever routine you are teaching him. Repeat the word associated with the act. Demonstrate again and again to give the dog a chance to make the connection in his mind.

Once he begins to get the idea, use the word of command without any physical guidance. Drill him. When he makes mistakes, correct him, kindly at first, more severely as his training progresses. Try not to lose your patience or become irritated, and never slap him with your hand or the leash during the training session. Withholding praise or rebuking him will make him feel bad enough.

When he does what you want, praise him lavishly with words and with pats. Don't continually reward with dog candy or treats in training. The dog that gets into the habit of performing for a treat will seldom be fully dependable when he can't smell or see one in the offing. When he carries out a command, even though his performance is slow or sloppy, praise him and he will perform more readily the next time.

THE TRAINING VOICE

When you start training your dog, use your training voice, giving commands in a firm, clear tone. Once you give a command, persist until it is obeyed, even if you have to pull the dog to obey you. He must learn that training is different from playing, that a command once given must be obeyed no matter what distractions are present. Remember that the tone and pitch of your voice, not loudness, are the qualities that will influence your dog most.

Be consistent in the use of words during training. Confine your commands to as few words as possible and never change them. It is best for only one person to carry on the dog's training, because different people will use different words and tactics that will confuse your dog. The dog who hears "*come,*" "*get over here,*" "*hurry up,*" "*here, Rex,*" and other commands when he is wanted will become totally confused.

TRAINING LESSONS

Training is hard on the dog — and on the trainer. A young dog just cannot take more than ten minutes of training at a stretch, so limit the length of your first lessons. Then you can gradually increase the length of time to about thirty minutes. You'll find that you too will tend to become impatient when you stretch out a training lesson. If you find yourself losing your temper, stop and resume the lesson at another time. Before and after each lesson have a play period, but don't play during a training session. Even the youngest dog soon learns that schooling is a serious matter; fun comes afterward.

Don't spend too much time on one phase of the training, or the dog will become bored. Always try to end a lesson on a pleasant note. Actually, in nine cases out of ten, if your dog isn't doing what you want it's because you're not getting the idea over to him properly.

YOUR TRAINING EQUIPMENT AND ITS USE

The leash is more properly called the lead, so we'll use that term here. The best leads for training are the six-foot webbed-cloth leads, usually olive-drab in color, and the six-foot leather lead. Fancier leads are available and may be used if desired.

You'll need a metal-link collar, called a choke chain, consisting of a metal chain with rings on each end. Even though the name may sound frightening, it won't hurt your dog, and it is an absolute MUST in training. There is a right and a wrong way to put the training collar on. It should go around the dog's neck so that you can attach the lead to the ring at the end of the chain which passes OVER, not under his neck. It is most important that the collar is put on properly so it will tighten when the lead is pulled and ease when you relax your grip.

The correct way to hold the lead is also very important, as the collar should have some slack in it, at all times, except when correcting. Holding the loop in your right hand, extend your arm out to the side, even with your shoulder. With your left hand, grasp the lead as close as possible to the collar, without making it tight. The remaining portion of the lead can be made into a loop which is held in the right hand. Keep this arm close to your body. Most corrections will be made with the left hand by giving the lead a jerk in the direction you want the dog to go. The dog that pulls and forges ahead can be corrected by a steady pull on the lead.

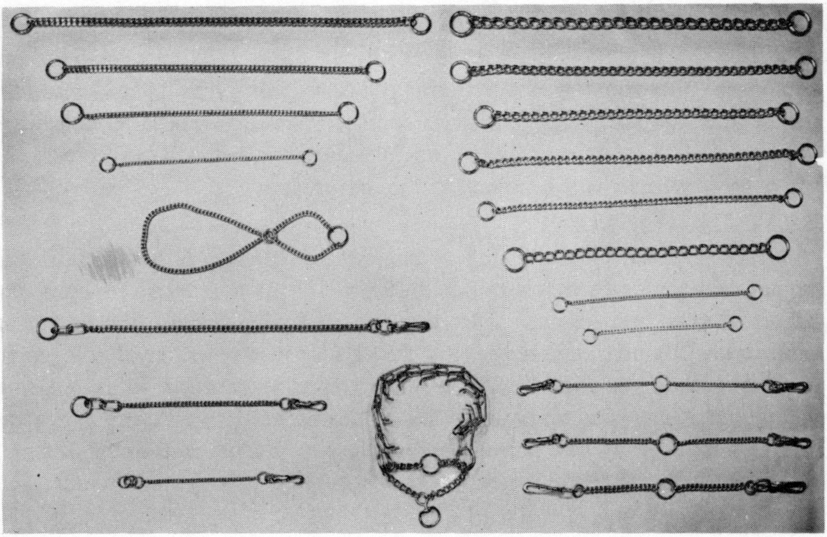

Special training collars for your dog can be purchased at your petshop.

HEELING

"*Heeling*" in dog language means having your dog walk alongside you on your left side, close to your leg, on lead or off. With patience and effort you can train your dog to walk with you even on a crowded street or in the presence of other dogs.

Now that you have learned the correct way to put on your dog's collar and how to hold the lead, you are ready to start with his first lesson in heeling. Put the dog at your left side, sitting. Using the dog's name and the command "*Heel,*" start forward on your LEFT foot, giving a tug on the lead to get the dog started. Always use the dog's name first, followed by the command, such as "*Rex, heel.*" Saying his name will help get his attention and will let him know that you are about to give a command.

Walk briskly, with even steps, going around in a large circle, square, or straight line. While walking, make sure that your dog stays on the left side and close to your leg. If he lags behind, give several tugs on the lead to get him up to you, then praise him for doing well. If he forges ahead or swings wide, stop and jerk the lead sharply and bring him back to the proper position. Always repeat the command when correcting, and praise him when he does well. If your dog continues to pull or lag behind, either your corrections are not severe enough or your timing between correction and praise is off. Do this exercise for only five minutes at first, gradually lengthening it to fifteen, or even half an hour.

To keep your dog's attention, talk to him as you keep him in place. You can also do a series of fast about-turns, giving the lead a jerk as you turn. He will gradually learn that he must pay attention or be jerked to your side. You can vary the routine by changing speeds, doing turns, figure-eights, and by zig-zagging across the training area.

"HEEL" MEANS "SIT," TOO

To the dog, the command "*Heel*" will also mean that he has to sit in the heel position at your left side when you stop walking — with no additional command from you. As you practice heeling, make him sit whenever you stop, at first using the word "*Sit,*" then with no command at all. He'll soon get the idea and sit down when you stop and wait for the command "*Heel*" to start walking again.

TRAINING TO SIT

Training your dog to sit should be fairly easy. Stand him on your left side, holding the lead fairly short, and command him to "*Sit.*" As you give the verbal command, pull up slightly with the lead and push his hindquarters down. Do not let him lie down or stand up. Keep him in a sitting position for a moment, then release the pressure on the lead and praise him. Constantly repeat the command as you hold him in a sitting position, thus fitting the word to the action in his mind. After a while he will begin to get the idea and will sit without your having to push his hindquarters down. When he reaches that stage, insist that he sit on command. If he is slow to obey, slap his hindquarters with your hand to get him down fast. *DO NOT HIT HIM HARD!* Teach him to sit on command facing you as well as when he is at your side. When he begins sitting on command with the lead on, try it with the lead off.

THE "LIE DOWN"

The object of this is to get the dog to lie down either on the verbal command "*Down*" or when you give him the hand signal, your hand raised in front of you, palm down. This is one of the most important parts of training. A well-trained dog will drop on command and stay down whatever the temptation: cat-chasing, car-chasing, or another dog across the street.

Don't start training to lie down until the dog is almost letter-perfect in sitting on command. Then place the dog in a sit, and kneel before him. With both hands, reach forward to his legs and take one front leg in each hand, thumbs up, and holding just below his elbows. Lift his legs slightly off the ground and pull them somewhat out in front of him. Simultaneously, give the command "*Down*" and lower his front legs to the ground.

Hold the dog down and stroke him to let him know that staying down is what you want him to do. This method is far better than forcing a young dog down. Using force can cause him to become very frightened and he will begin to dislike any training. Always talk to your dog and let him know that you are very pleased with him, and soon you will find that you have a happy working dog.

After he begins to get the idea, slide the lead under your left foot and give the command "*Down.*" At the same time, pull the lead. This will help get the dog down. Meanwhile, raise your hand in the down signal. Don't expect to accomplish all this in one session. Be patient and work with the dog. He'll cooperate if you show him just what you expect him to do.

THE "STAY"

The next step is to train your dog to stay either in a "*Sit*" or "*Down*" position. Sit him at your side. Give the command "*Stay,*" but be careful not to use his name with this command, because hearing his name may lead him to think that some action is expected of him. If he begins to move, repeat "*Stay*" firmly and hold him down in the sit. Constantly repeat the word "*Stay*" to fix the meaning of that command in his mind. After he has learned to stay for a short time, gradually increase the length of his stay. The hand signal for the stay is a downward sweep of your hand toward the dog's nose, with the palm facing him. While he is sitting, walk around him and stand in front of him. Hold the lead at first; later, drop the lead on the ground in front of him and keep him sitting. If he bolts, scold him and place him back in the same position, repeating the command and all the exercise.

Use some word such as "*Okay*" or "*Up*" to let him know when he can get up, and praise him well for a good performance. As this practice continues, walk farther and farther away from him. Later, try sitting him, giving the command to stay, and then walk out of sight, first for a few seconds, then for longer periods. A well-trained dog should stay where you put him without moving until you come and release him.

Similarly, practice having him stay in the down position, first with you near him, later when you step out of sight.

THE "COME" ON COMMAND

You can train your dog to come when you call him, if you begin when he is young. At first, work with him on lead. Sit the dog, then back away the length of the lead and call him, putting into your voice as much coaxing affection as possible. Give an easy tug on the lead to get him started. When he does come, make a big fuss over him; it might help at this point to give him a small piece of dog candy or food as a reward. He should get the idea soon. You can also move away from him the full length of the lead and call to him something like "*Rex, come,*" then run backward a few steps and stop, making him sit directly in front of you.

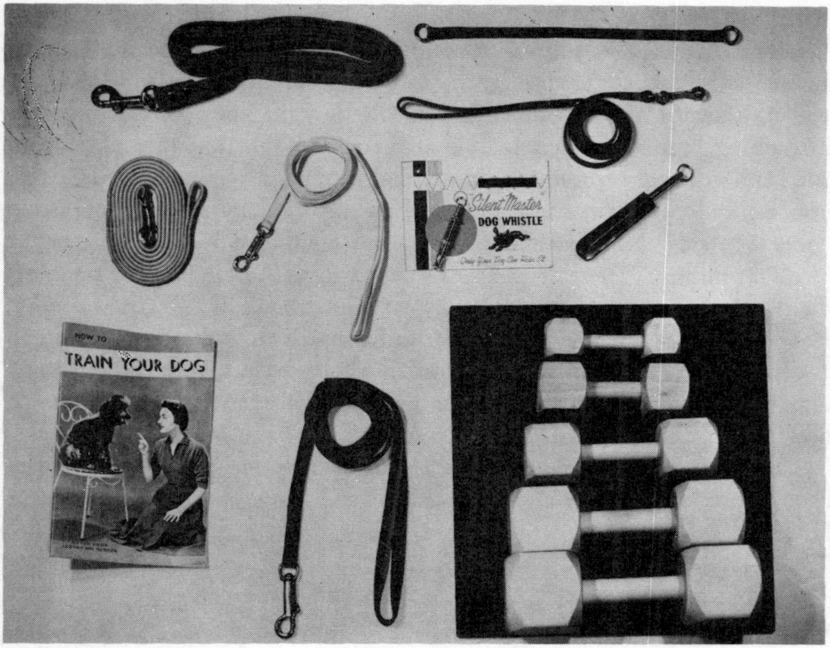

Visit your petshop for all of the training equipment you will need to make your pet a better canine citizen.

Don't be too eager to practice coming on command off lead. Wait until you are certain that you have the dog under perfect control before you try calling him when he's free. Once he gets the idea that he can disobey a command and get away with it, your training program will suffer a serious setback. Keep in mind that your dog's life may depend on his immediate response to a command to come when he is called. If he disobeys off lead, put the lead back on and correct him severely with jerks of the lead.

TEACHING TO COME TO HEEL

The object of this is for you to stand still, say "*Heel,*" and have your dog come right over to you and sit by your left knee in the heel position. If your dog has been trained to sit without command every time you stop, he's ready for this step.

Sit him in front of and facing you and step back one step. Moving only your left foot, pull the dog behind you, then step forward and pull him around until he is in a heel position. You can also have the dog go around by passing the lead behind your back. Use your left heel to straighten him out if he begins to sit behind you or crookedly. This may take a little work, but he will get the idea if you show him just what you want.

THE "STAND"

Your dog should be trained to stand in one spot without moving his feet, and he should allow a stranger to run his hand over his body and legs without showing any resentment or fear. Employ the same method you used in training him to stay on the sit and down. While walking, place your left hand out, palm toward his nose, and command him to stay. His first impulse will be to sit, so be prepared to stop him by placing your hand under his body, near his hindquarters, and holding him until he gets the idea that this is different from the command to sit. Praise him for standing, then walk to the end of the lead. Correct him strongly if he starts to move. Have a stranger approach him and run his hands over the dog's back and down his legs. Keep him standing until you come back to him. Walk around him from his left side, come to the heel position, and make sure that he does not sit until you command him to.

This is a very valuable exercise. If you plan to show your dog he will have learned to stand in a show pose and will allow the judge to examine him.

TRAINING SCHOOLS AND CLASSES

There are dog-training classes in all parts of the country, some sponsored by the local humane society.

If you feel that you lack the time or the skill to train your dog yourself, there are professional dog trainers who will do it for you, but basically dog training is a matter of training YOU and your dog to work together as a team, and if you don't do it yourself you will miss a lot of fun. Don't give up after trying unsuccessfully for a short time. Try a little harder and you and your dog will be able to work things out.

ADVANCED TRAINING AND OBEDIENCE TRIALS

Once you begin training your dog and you see how well he does, you'll probably be bitten by the "obedience bug" — the desire to enter him in obedience trials held under American Kennel Club auspices.

The A.K.C. obedience trials are divided into three classes: Novice, Open, and Utility.

In the Novice Class, the dog will be judged on the following basis:

TEST	MAXIMUM SCORE
Heel on lead	35
Stand for examination	30
Heel free — off lead	45
Recall (come on command)	30
One-minute sit (handler in ring)	30
Three-minute down (handler in ring)	30
Maximum total score	200

If the dog "qualifies" in three shows by earning at least 50% of the points for each test, with a total of at least 170 for the trial, he has earned the Companion Dog degree and the letters C.D. (Companion Dog) are entered after his name in the A.K.C. records.

After the dog has qualified as a C.D., he is eligible to enter the Open Class competition, where he will be judged on this basis:

TEST	MAXIMUM SCORE
Heel free	40
Drop on Recall	30
Retrieve (wooden dumbbell) on flat	25
Retrieve over obstacle (hurdle)	35
Broad jump	20
Three-minute sit (handler out of ring)	25
Five-minute down (handler out of ring)	25
Maximum total score	200

Again he must qualify in three shows for the C.D.X. (Companion Dog Excellent) title and then is eligible for the Utility Class, where he can earn the Utility Dog (U.D.) degree in these rugged tests:

TEST	MAXIMUM SCORE
Scent discrimination (picking up article handled by master from group) Article 1	20
Scent discrimination Article 2	20
Scent discrimination Article 3	20
Seek back (picking up an article dropped by handler)	30
Signal exercise (heeling, etc., on hand signal)	35
Directed jumping (over hurdle and bar jump)	40
Group examination	35
Maximum total score	200

For more complete information about these obedience trials, write for the American Kennel Club's *Regulations and Standards for Obedience Trials*. Dogs that are disqualified from breed shows because of alteration or physical defects are eligible to compete in these trials. Besides the formal A.K.C. obedience trials, there are informal "match" shows in which dogs compete for ribbons and inexpensive trophies. These shows are run by many local fanciers' dog clubs and by all-breed obedience clubs. In many localities the humane society and other groups conduct their own obedience shows. Your local petshop or kennel can keep you informed about such shows in your vicinity, and you will find them listed in the different dog magazines or in the pet column of your local newspaper.

6. Breeding

THE QUESTION OF SPAYING

If you feel that you will never want to raise a litter of purebred puppies, and if you do not wish to risk the possibility of an undesirable mating and surplus mongrel puppies inevitably destined for execution at the local pound, you may want to have your female spayed. Spaying is generally best performed after the female has passed her first heat and before her first birthday: this allows the female to attain the normal female characteristics, while still being young enough to avoid the possible complications encountered when an older female is spayed. A spayed female will remain a healthy, lively pet. You often hear that an altered female will become very fat. However, if you cut down on her food intake, she will not gain weight.

On the other hand, if you wish to show your dog (altered females are disqualified) or enjoy the excitement and feeling of accomplishment of breeding and raising a litter of puppies, particularly in your breed and from your pet, then definitely do not spay.

Male dogs, unlike tomcats, are almost never altered (castrated).

SEXUAL PHYSIOLOGY

Females usually reach sexual maturity (indicated by the first heat cycle, or season) at eight or nine months of age, but sexual maturity may occur as early as six months or as late as thirteen months of age. The average heat cycle (estrus period) lasts for twenty or twenty-one days, and occurs approximately every six months. For about five days immediately preceding the heat period, the female generally displays restlessness and an increased appetite. The vulva, or external genitals, begin to swell. The discharge, which is bright red at the onset and gradually becomes pale pink to straw in color, increases in quantity for several days and then slowly subsides, finally ceasing altogether. The vaginal discharge is subject to much variation: in some bitches it is quite heavy, in others it may never appear, and in some it may be so slight as to go unnoticed.

About eight or nine days after the first appearance of the discharge, the female becomes very playful with other dogs, but will not allow a mating to take place. Anywhere from the tenth or eleventh day, when the discharge has virtually ended and the vulva has softened, to the seventeenth or eighteenth day, the female will accept males and be able to conceive. Many biologists apply the term "heat" only to this receptive phase rather than to the whole estrus, as is commonly done by dog fanciers.

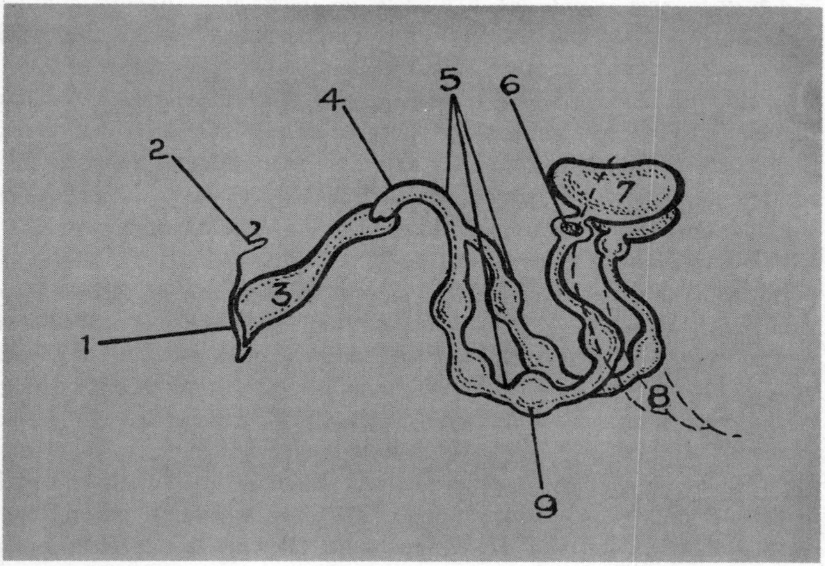

The reproduction system of the bitch: 1, vulva; 2, anus; 3, vagina; 4, cervix; 5, uterus; 6, ovary; 7, kidneys; 8, ribs; 9, fetal lump.

The ova (egg cells) from the female's ovaries are discharged into the oviduct toward the close of the acceptance phase, usually from the sixteenth to eighteenth day. From the eighteenth day until the end of the cycle, the female is still attractive to males, but she will repulse their advances. The entire estrus, however, may be quite variable: in some females vaginal bleeding ends and mating begins on the fourth day; in others, the discharge may continue throughout the entire cycle and the female will not accept males until the seventeenth day or even later.

The male dog — simply referred to by fanciers as the "dog," in contrast to the female, which is referred to as the "bitch" — upon reaching sexual maturity, usually at about six to eight months, is able, like other domesticated mammals, to breed at any time throughout the year.

The testes, the sperm-producing organs of the male, descend from the body cavity into the scrotum at birth. The condition of *cryptorchidism* refers to the retention of one or both testes within the body cavity. A testicle retained within the body cavity is in an environment too hot for it to function normally. A retained testicle may also become cancerous. If only one testicle descends, the dog is known as a *monorchid;* if neither descends, the dog is known as an *anorchid* (dog fanciers, however, refer to a dog with the latter condition as a cryptorchid). A monorchid dog is a fertile animal; an anorchid is sterile.

The male dog's penis has a bulbous enlargement at its base and, in addition, like the penis of a number of other mammals, contains a bone. When mating occurs, pressure on the penis causes a reflex action that fills the bulb with blood, swelling it to about five times its normal size within the female. This locks, or ties, the two animals together. After ejaculation, the animals usually remain tied for fifteen to thirty minutes, but they may separate very quickly or remain together an hour or more, depending on the length of time it takes for the blood to drain from the bulb.

CARE OF THE FEMALE IN ESTRUS

If you have a dog-proof run within your yard, it will be safe to leave your female in season there; if you don't have such a run, she should be shut indoors. Don't leave her alone outside even for a minute; she should be exercised only on lead. If you want to prevent the neighborhood dogs from congregating around your doorstep, as they inevitably will as soon as they discover that your female is in season, take her some distance from the house before you let her relieve herself. Take her in your car to a park or field for a chance to "stretch" her legs (always on lead of course). Keep watch for male dogs, and if one approaches take the female back to the car. After the three weeks are up you can let her out as before with no worry that she can have puppies until her next season.

Some owners find it simpler to board their female at a kennel until her season is over. However, it really is not difficult to watch your female at home. There are various products on the market which are useful at this time. Although the female in season keeps herself quite clean, sometimes she unavoidably stains furniture or rugs. You can buy sanitary belts made especially for dogs at your petshop. Consult your veterinarian for information on pills to be taken to check odor during this period. There also is a pill that prevents the female from coming in season for extended periods, and there are many different types of liquids, powders, and sprays of varying efficiency used to keep male dogs away. However, the one safe rule (whatever products you use) is: keep your bitch away from dogs that could mount her.

SHOULD YOU BREED YOUR MALE?

As with every question, whether or not to use a male dog as a stud has two sides. The arguments for and against using a dog as a stud are often very close to the ridiculous. A classic example would be the tale that once you use a dog as a stud he will lose his value as a show dog or any one of the other functions a dog may have. A sound rule may well be: *if you have a stud who has proven his worth at the shows, place his services out for hire, if only for the betterment of the breed; if your dog is not of show quality, do not use him as a stud.*

Top champion studs can bring their owners many dollars in breeding revenue. If the stud is as good as you feel he is, his services will soon be in great demand. Using a dog as a stud will not lower his value in other functions in any way. Many breeders will permit a male dog to breed an experienced female once, when about a year old, and then they begin to show their stud until he has gained his conformation championship. He is then placed out for hire through advertising in the various bulletins, journals, and show catalogs, and through the stud registers maintained by many petshops.

SHOULD YOU BREED YOUR FEMALE?

If you are an amateur and decide to breed your female it would be wise to talk with a breeder and find out all that breeding and caring for puppies entails. You must be prepared to assume the responsibility of caring for the mother through her pregnancy and for the puppies until they are of saleable age. Raising a litter of puppies can be a rewarding experience, but it means work as well as fun, and there is no guarantee of financial profit. As the puppies grow older and require more room and care, the amateur breeder, in desperation, often sells the puppies for much less than they are worth; sometimes he has to give them away. If the cost of keeping the puppies will drain your finances, think twice.

If you have given careful consideration to all these things and still want to breed your female, remember that there is some preparation necessary before taking this step.

WHEN TO BREED

It is usually best to breed in the second or third season. Consider when the puppies will be born and whether their birth and later care will interfere with your work or vacation plans. Gestation period is approximately fifty-eight to sixty-three days. Allow enough time to select the right stud for her. Don't be in a position of having to settle for any available male if she comes into season sooner than expected. Your female will probably be ready to breed twelve days after the first colored discharge. You can usually make arrangements to board her with the owner of the male for a few days to insure her being there at the proper time, or you can take her to be mated and bring her home the same day. If she still appears receptive she may be bred again a day or two later. Some females never show signs of willingness, so it helps to have the experience of a breeder. The second day after the discharge changes color is the proper time; she may be bred for about three days following. For an additional week or so she may have some discharge and attract other dogs by her odor, but she can seldom be bred at this time.

HOW TO SELECT A STUD

Choose a mate for your female with an eye to countering her deficiencies. If possible, both male and female should have several ancestors in common within the last two or three generations, as such combinations generally "click" best. The male should have a good show record himself or be the sire of champions. The owner of the stud usually charges a fee for the use of the dog. The fee varies. Payment of a fee does not guarantee a litter, but it does generally confer the right to breed your female again to the stud if she does not have puppies the first time. In some cases the owner of the stud will agree to take a choice puppy in place of a stud fee. You and the owner of the stud should settle all details beforehand, including such questions as what age the puppies should reach before the stud's owner can make his choice, what disposition is made of a single surviving puppy under an agreement by which the stud owner has pick of the litter, and so on. In all cases it is best that the agreement entered into by bitch owner and stud owner be in the form of a written contract.

It is customary for the female to be sent to the male; if the stud dog of your choice lives any distance you will have to make arrangements to have your female shipped to him. The quickest way is by air, and if you call your nearest airport the airline people will give you information as to the best and fastest flight. Some airlines furnish their own crates for shipping, whereas others require that you furnish your own. The owner of the stud will make the arrangements for shipping the female back to you. You have to pay all shipping charges.

PREPARATION FOR BREEDING

Before you breed your female, make sure she is in good health. She should be neither too thin nor too fat. Skin diseases must be cured before breeding; a bitch with skin diseases can pass them on to her puppies. If she has worms she should be wormed before being bred, or within three weeks afterward. It is a good idea to have your veterinarian give her a booster shot for distemper and hepatitis before the puppies are born. This will increase the immunity the puppies receive during their early, most vulnerable period. Choose a dependable veterinarian and rely on him if there is an emergency when your female whelps.

HOW OFTEN SHOULD YOU BREED YOUR FEMALE?

Do not breed your bitch after she reaches six years of age. If you wish to breed her several times while she is young, it is wise to breed her only once a year. In other words, breed her, skip a season, and then breed her again. This will allow her to gain back her full strength between whelpings.

THE IMPORTANCE AND APPLICATION OF GENETICS

Any person attempting to breed dogs should have a basic understanding of the transmission of traits, or characteristics, from the parents to the offspring and some familiarity with the more widely used genetic terms that he will probably encounter. A knowledge of the fundamental mechanics of genetics enables a breeder to better comprehend the passing, complementing, and covering of both good points and faults from generation to generation. It enables him to make a more judicial and scientific decision in selecting potential mates.

Inheritance, fundamentally, is due to the existence of microscopic units, known as *GENES,* present in the cells of all individuals. Genes somehow control the biochemical reactions that occur within the embryo or adult organism. This control results in changing or guiding the development of the organism's characteristics. A "string" of attached genes is known as a *CHROMOSOME.* With a few important exceptions, every chromosome has a partner chromosome carrying a duplicate or equivalent set of genes. Each gene, therefore, has a partner gene, known as an *ALLELE.* The number of different pairs of chromosomes present in the cells of the organism varies with the type of organism: a certain parasitic worm has only one pair, a certain fruit fly has four different pairs, man has 23 different pairs, and your dog has 39 different pairs per cell. Because each chromosome may have many hundreds of genes, a single cell of the body may contain a total of several thousand genes. Heredity is obviously a very complex matter.

In the simplest form of genetic inheritance, one particular gene and its duplicate, or allele, on the partner chromosome control a single characteristic. The presence of freckles in the human skin, for example, is believed to be due to the influence of a single pair of genes.

Each cell of the body contains the specific number of paired chromosomes characteristic of the organism. Because each type of gene is present on both chromosomes of a chromosome pair, *each type of gene is therefore present in duplicate.* The fusion of a sperm cell from the male with an egg cell from the female, as occurs in fertilization, should therefore result in offspring having a *quadruplicate number* (4) of each type of gene. Mating of these individuals would then produce progeny having an *octuplicate number* (8) of each type of gene, and so on. This, however, is normally prevented by a special process. When ordinary body cells prepare to divide to form more tissue, each pair of chromosomes duplicates itself so that there are four partner chromosomes of each kind instead of only two. When the cell divides, two of the four partners, or one pair, go into each new cell. This process, known as *MITOSIS,* insures that each new body cell contains the proper number of chromosomes. Reproductive cells (sperm cell and egg cells), however, undergo a special kind of division known as *MEIOSIS.* In meiosis, the chromosome pairs do *not* duplicate themselves, and thus when the reproductive cells reach the final dividing stage only one chromosome, or one-half of the pair, goes into each new reproductive cell. Each reproductive cell, therefore, has only half the normal number of chromosomes. These are referred to as *HAPLOID* cells, in contrast to *DIPLOID* cells, which have the full number of chromosomes.

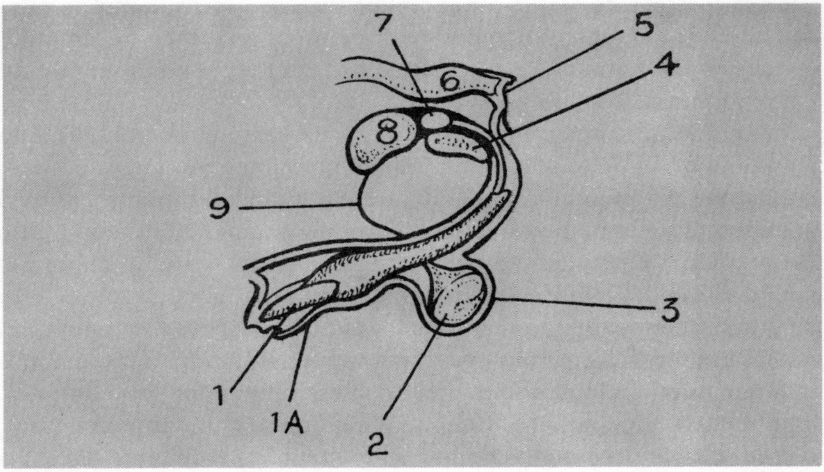

The reproductive system of a male: 1a, sheath; 1, penis; 2, testicle; 3, scrotum; 4, pelvic bone; 5, anus; 6, rectum; 7, prostate; 8, bladder; 9, vas deferens.

When the haploid sperm cell fuses with the haploid egg cell in fertilization, the resulting offspring has the normal diploid number of chromosomes.

If both partner genes, or alleles, affect the trait in an identical manner, the genes are said to be *HOMOZYGOUS,* but if one affects the character in a manner different from the other gene, or allele, the genes are said to be *HETEROZYGOUS*. For example, in the pair of genes affecting eye color in humans, if each gene of the pair produces blue eyes, the genes (and also the person carrying the genes) are said to be homozygous for blue eyes. If, however, one gene of the pair produces blue eyes, while the other gene, or allele, produces brown eyes, they are said to be heterozygous. The presence of heterozygous genes raises the question, "*Will the offspring have blue eyes or brown eyes?*" which in turn introduces another genetic principle: *DOMINANCE* and *RECESSIVENESS*.

If one gene of a pair can block the action of its partner, or allele, while still producing its own affect, that gene is said to be *dominant* over its allele. Its allele, on the other hand, is said to be recessive. In the case of heterozygous genes for eye color, the brown eye gene is dominant over the recessive blue eye gene, and the offspring therefore will have brown eyes. Much less common is the occurrence of gene pairs in which neither gene is completely dominant over the other. This, known as *INCOMPLETE* or *PARTIAL DOMINANCE,* results in a blending of the opposing influences. In cattle, if a homozygous (pure) red bull is mated with a homozygous (pure) white cow, the calf will be roan, a blending of red and white hairs in its coat, rather than either all red or all white.

During meiosis, or division of the reproductive (sperm and egg) cells, each pair of chromosomes splits, and one-half of each pair goes into one of the two new cells. Thus, in the case of eye color genes, one new reproductive cell will get the chromosome carrying the blue eye gene, while the other new reproductive cell will get the chromosome carrying the brown eye gene, and so on for each pair of chromosomes. If an organism has only two pairs of chromosomes — called pair A, made up of chromosomes A_1 and A_2, and pair B, made up of chromosomes B_1 and B_2 — each new reproductive cell will get one chromosome from each pair, and four different combinations are possible: A_1 and B_1; A_1 and B_2; A_2 and B_1, or A_2 and B_2. If the blue eye gene is on A_1, the brown eye gene on A_2, the gene for curly hair on B_1 and the gene for straight hair on B_2, each of the above combinations will exert a different genetic effect on the offspring. This different grouping of chromosomes in the new reproductive cell as a result of meiotic cell division is known as *INDEPENDENT ASSORTMENT* and is one reason why variation occurs in the offspring. In the dog, with 39 pairs of chromosomes, the possibilities of variation through independent assortment are tremendous.

But variation does not end here. For example, if two dominant genes, such as the genes for brown eyes and dark hair, were on the same chromosome, all brown-eyed people would have dark hair. Yet in instances where such joined or *LINKED* genes do occur, the two characteristics do not always appear together in the same offspring. This is due to a process known as *CROSS-OVER* or *RECOMBINATION*. Recombination is the mutual exchange of corresponding blocks of genes between the two chromosomes in a pair. That is, during cell division, the two chromosomes may exchange their tip sections or other corresponding segments. If the segments exchanged contain the eye color genes, the brown eye gene will be transferred from the chromosome carrying the dark hair gene to the chromosome carrying the light hair gene, and then brown eyes will occur with light hair, provided that the individual is homozygous for the recessive light hair gene.

Another important source of variation is *MUTATION*. In mutation, a gene becomes altered, such as by exposure to irradiation, and exerts a different effect than it did before. Most mutations are harmful to the organism, and some may result in death. Offspring carrying mutated genes and showing the effects of these mutations are known as *MUTANTS* or *SPORTS*. Mutation also means that instead of only two alleles for eye color, such as brown and blue, there may now be three or more (gray, black, etc.) creating a much larger source for possible variation in the offspring.

Further complications in the transmission and appearance of genetic traits are the phenomena known as *EPISTASIS* and *PLEIOTROPY*. Epistasis refers to a gene exerting influence on genes other than its own allele.

In all-white red-eyed (albino) guinea pigs, for example, the gene controlling intensity of color is epistatic to any other color gene and prevents that gene from producing its effect. Thus, even if a gene for red spots were present in the cells of the guinea pig, the color intensity gene would prevent the red spots from appearing in the guinea pig's white coat. *Pleiotropy* refers to the fact that a single gene may control a number of characteristics. In the fruit fly, for example, the gene that controls eye color may also affect the structure of certain body parts and even the lifespan of the insect.

One special pair of chromosomes is known as the sex chromosomes. In man, dog, and other mammals, these chromosomes are of two types, designated as X and Y. Under normal conditions, a mammal carrying two X-type sex chromosomes is a female, whereas a mammal carrying one X-type and one Y-type is a male. Females, therefore, have only X chromosomes and can only contribute X chromosomes to the offspring, but the male may contribute either an X or a Y.

If the male's sperm carrying an X chromosome fertilizes the female's egg cell (X), the offspring (XX) will be female; if a sperm carrying a Y chromosome fertilizes the egg (X), the offspring (XY) will be male. It is the male, therefore, that determines the sex of the offspring in mammals.

Traits controlled by genes present on the sex chromosome, and which appear in only one sex, are said to be *SEX LINKED*. If, for example, a rare recessive gene occurs on the X chromosome, it cannot exert its effect in the female because the dominant allele on the other X chromosome will counteract it. In the male, however, there is no second X chromosome, and if the Y chromosome cannot offer any countereffect, the recessive character will appear. There are also *SEX-LIMITED* characteristics: these appear primarily or solely in one sex, but the genes for these traits are not carried on the sex chromosomes. Sex-limited traits appear when genes on other chromosomes exert their effect in the proper hormonal (male or female) environment. Sex-linked and sex-limited transmission is how a trait may skip a generation, by being passed from grandfather to grandson through a mother in which the trait, though present, does not show.

In dealing with the simplest form of heredity — one gene effecting one character — there is an expected ratio of the offspring displaying the character to those who do not display it, depending upon the genetic makeup of the parents. If a parent is homozygous for a character, such as blue eyes, it makes no difference which half of the chromosome pair enters the new reproductive cell, because each chromosome carries the gene for blue eyes. If a parent is heterozygous, however, one reproductive cell will receive the brown eye gene while the other will receive the blue eye gene. If both parents are homozygous for blue eyes, all the offspring will receive two blue eye genes, and all will have blue eyes. If a parent is homozygous for blue eyes, and the other parent is homozygous for brown eyes, all the offspring will be heterozygous, receiving one brown eye gene and one blue eye gene, and because brown is dominant, all will have brown eyes. If both parents are heterozygous, both the blue eye gene and the brown eye gene from one parent have an equal likelihood of ending up with either the blue eye or the brown eye gene from the other parent. This results in a ratio of two heterozygous offspring to the one homozygous for brown eyes and one homozygous for blue eyes, giving a total genetic, or genotypic, ratio of 2:1:1 or, as it is more commonly arranged, 1:2:1. As the two heterozygous as well as the homozygous brown eye offspring will have brown eyes, the ratio of brown eyes to blue eyes (or phenotypic ratio) will be 3:1.

If one parent is heterozygous and the other parent is homozygous for the recessive gene for blue eyes, half of the offspring will be homozygous for blue eyes and will have blue eyes, but the other half of the offspring will be heterozygous and have brown eyes. (Here both the genotypic and phenotypic ratio is 1:1.)

If the homozygous parent, however, has the dominant gene (brown eyes), half of the offspring will be heterozygous and half will be homozygous, as before, but all will have brown eyes. By repeated determinations of these ratios in the offspring, geneticists are able to analyze the genetic makeup of the parents.

Before leaving heredity, it might be well to explain the difference between inbreeding, outcrossing, line breeding, and similar terms. Basically, there are only inbreeding and outbreeding. Inbreeding, however, according to its intensity, is usually divided into inbreeding proper and line breeding. Inbreeding proper is considered to be the mating of very closely related individuals, generally within the immediate family, but this is sometimes extended to include matings to first cousins and grandparents. Line breeding is the mating of more distantly related animals, that is, animals, not immediately related to each other but having a common ancestor, such as the same grandsire or great-grandsire. Outbreeding is divided into outcrossing, which is the mating of dogs from different families within the same breed, and cross-breeding, which is mating purebred dogs from different breeds.

From the foregoing discussion of genetics, it should be realized that the theory of telegony, which states that the sire of one litter can influence future litters sired by other studs, is simply not true; it is possible, however, if several males mate with a female during a single estrus cycle, that the various puppies in the litter may have different sires (but not two sires for any one puppy). It should also be realized that blood does not really enter into the transmission of inheritance, although people commonly speak of "bloodlines," "pure-blooded," etc.

7. Care of the Mother and Family

PRENATAL CARE OF THE FEMALE

You can expect the puppies nine weeks from the day of breeding, although 58 days is as common as 63. During this time the female should receive normal care and exercise. If she is overweight, don't increase her food at first; excess weight at whelping time is not good. If she is on the thin side, build her up, giving her a morning meal of cereal and egg yolk. Consult your veterinarian as to increasing her vitamins and mineral supplement. During the last weeks the puppies grow enormously, and the mother will have little room for food and less appetite. Divide her meals into smaller portions and feed her more ofen. If she loses her appetite, tempt her with meat, liver, chicken, etc.

As she grows heavier, eliminate violent exercise and jumping. Do not eliminate exercise entirely, as walking is beneficial to the female in whelp, and mild exercise will maintain her muscle tone in preparation for the birth. Weigh your female after breeding and keep a record of her weight each week thereafter. Groom your bitch daily — some females have a slight discharge during gestation, more prevalent during the last two weeks, so wash the vulva with warm water daily. Usually, by the end of the fifth week you can notice a broadening across her loins, and her breasts become firmer. By the end of the sixth week your veterinarian can tell you whether or not she is pregnant.

PREPARATION OF WHELPING QUARTERS

Prepare a whelping box at least a week before the puppies are to arrive and allow the mother-to-be to sleep there overnight or to spend some time in it during the day to become accustomed to it. She is then less likely to try to have her litter under the front porch or in the middle of your bed.

The box should have a wooden floor. Sides should be high enough to keep the puppies in but low enough to allow the mother to get out after she has fed them. Layers of newspapers spread over the whole area will make excellent bedding and will be absorbent enough to keep the surface warm and dry. They should be removed when wet or soiled and replaced with another thick layer. An old quilt or blanket is more comfortable for the mother and makes better footing for the nursing puppies, at least during the first week, than slippery newspaper. The quilt should be secured firmly.

SUPPLIES TO HAVE ON HAND

As soon as you have the whelping box prepared, set up the nursery by collecting the various supplies you will need when the puppies arrive. You should have the following items on hand: a box lined with towels for the puppies, a heating pad or hot water bottle to keep the puppy box warm, a pile of clean terrycloth towels or washcloths to remove membranes and to dry puppies, a stack of folded newspapers, a roll of paper towels, vaseline, rubber gloves, soap, iodine, muzzle, cotton balls, a small pair of blunt scissors to cut umbilical cords (stick them into an open bottle of alcohol so they keep freshly sterilized), a rectal thermometer, white thread, a flashlight in case the electricity goes off, a waste container, and a scale for weighing each puppy at birth.

It is necessary that the whelping room be warm and free from drafts, because puppies are delivered wet from the mother. Keep a little notebook and pencil handy so you can record the duration of the first labor and the time between the arrival of each puppy. If there is trouble in whelping, this is the information that the veterinarian will want. Keep his telephone number handy in case you have to call him in an emergency, and warn him to be prepared for an emergency, should you need him.

WHELPING

Be prepared for the actual whelping several days in advance. Usually the female will tear up papers, try to dig nests, refuse food, and generally act restless and nervous. These may be false alarms; the real test is her temperature, which will drop to below 100° about twelve hours before whelping. Take her temperature rectally at a set time each day, starting about a week before she is due to whelp. After her temperature goes down, keep her constantly with you or put her in the whelping box and stay in the room with her. She will seem anxious and look to you for reassurance. Be prepared to remove the membranes covering the puppy's head if the mother fails to do this, for the puppy could smother otherwise.

The mother should start licking the puppy as soon as it is out of the sac, thus drying and stimulating it, but if she does not perform this task you can do it with a soft rough towel, instead. The afterbirth should follow the birth of each puppy, attached to the puppy by the umbilical cord. Watch to make sure that each is expelled, for retaining this material can cause infection. The mother probably will eat the afterbirth after biting the cord. One or two will not hurt her; they stimulate milk supply as well as labor for remaining puppies. Too many, however, can make her lose her appetite for the food she needs to feed her puppies and regain her strength, so remove the rest of them along with the soiled newspapers, and keep the box dry and clean to relieve her anxiety.

If a puppy does not start breathing, wrap him in a towel, hold him upside down with his head toward the ground, and shake him vigorously. If he still does not breathe, rub his ribs briskly; if this also fails, administer artificial respiration by compressing the ribs about twenty times per minute.

If the mother does not bite the cord, or bites it too close to the body, you should take over the job to prevent an umbilical hernia. Cut the cord a short distance from the body with your blunt scissors. Put a drop of iodine on the end of the cord; it will dry up and fall off in a few days.

The puppies should follow each other at regular intervals, but deliveries can be as short as five minutes or as long as two hours apart. A puppy may be presented backwards; if the mother does not seem to be in trouble, do not interfere. But if enough of the puppy is outside the birth canal, use a rough towel and help her by pulling gently on the puppy. Pull only when she pushes. A rear-first, or breech, birth can cause a puppy to strangle on its own umbilical cord, so don't let the mother struggle too long. Breech birth is quite common.

When you think all the puppies have been whelped, have your veterinarian examine the mother to determine if all the afterbirths have been expelled. He will probably give her an injection to be certain that the uterus is clean, a shot of calcium for prevention of eclampsia, and possibly an injection of penicillin to prevent infection.

RAISING THE PUPPIES

Hold each puppy to a breast as soon as you have dried him. This will be an opportunity to have a good meal without competition. Then place him in the small box that you have prepared so he will be out of his mother's way while she is whelping. Keep a record of birth weights and take weekly readings thereafter so that you will have an accurate account of the puppies' growth. After the puppies have arrived, take the mother outside for a walk and a drink, and then leave her to take care of them. Offer her a dish of vanilla ice cream or milk with corn syrup in it. She usually will eat lying down while the puppies are nursing and will appreciate the coolness of the ice cream during warm weather or in a hot room. She will not want to stay away from her puppies more than a minute or two the first few weeks. Be sure to keep water available at all times, and feed her milk or broth frequently, as she needs liquids to produce milk. To encourage her to eat, offer her the foods she likes best, until she "asks" to be fed without your tempting her. She will soon develop a ravenous appetite and should be fed whenever she is hungry.

Be sure that all the puppies are getting enough to eat. Cut their claws with special dog "nail" clippers, as they grow rapidly and scratch the mother as the puppies nurse. Normally the puppies should be completely weaned by six weeks, although you may start to give them supplementary feedings at three weeks. They will find it easier to lap semi-solid food.

As the puppies grow up, the mother will go into the box only to nurse them, first sitting up and then standing. To dry up her milk supply completely, keep her away from her puppies for longer periods. After a few days of part-time nursing she will be able to stay away for much longer periods of time, and then completely. The little milk left will be resorbed.

When the puppies are five weeks old, consult your veterinarian about temporary shots to protect them against distemper and hepatitis; it is quite possible for dangerous infectious germs to reach them even though you keep their living quarters sanitary. You can expect the puppies to need at least one worming before they are ready to go to their new homes, so take a stool sample to your veterinarian before they are three weeks old. If one puppy has worms, all should be wormed. Follow your veterinarian's advice.

The puppies may be put outside, unless it is too cold, as soon as their eyes are open (about ten days), and they will benefit from the sunlight. A rubber mat or newspapers underneath their box will protect them from cold or dampness.

HOW TO TAKE CARE OF A LARGE LITTER

The size of a litter varies greatly. If your bitch has a large litter she may have trouble feeding all of the puppies. You can help her by preparing an extra puppy box. Leave half the litter with the mother and the other half in a warm place, changing their places at two-hour intervals at first. Later you may change them less frequently, leaving them all together except during the day. Try supplementary feeding, too, as soon as their eyes are open.

CAESAREAN SECTION

If your female goes into hard labor and is not able to give birth within two hours, you will know that there is something wrong. Call your veterinarian for advice. Some females must have Caesarean sections (taking puppies from the mother by surgery), but don't be alarmed if your dog has to undergo this. The operation is relatively safe. She can be taken to the veterinarian, operated on, and then be back in her whelping box at home within three hours, with all puppies nursing normally a short time later.

8. Health

WATCHING YOUR PUPPY'S HEALTH

First, don't be frightened by the number of diseases a dog can contract. The majority of dogs never get any of them. Don't become a dog-hypochondriac. All dogs have days when they feel lazy and want to lie around doing nothing. For the few diseases that you might be concerned about, remember that your veterinarian is your dog's best friend. When you first get your puppy, select a veterinarian who you feel is qualified to treat dogs. He will get to know your dog and will be glad to have you consult him for advice. A dog needs little medical care, but that little is essential to his good health and well-being. He needs:

1. Proper diet at regular hours
2. Clean, roomy housing
3. Daily exercise
4. Companionship and love
5. Frequent grooming
6. Regular check-ups by your veterinarian

THE USEFUL THERMOMETER

Almost every serious ailment shows itself by an increase in the dog's body temperature. If your dog acts lifeless, looks dull-eyed, and gives the impression of illness, check his temperature by using a rectal thermometer. Hold the dog and insert the thermometer, which should be lubricated with vaseline, and take a reading. The average normal temperature is 101.5° F. Excitement may raise this value slightly, but any rise of more than a few points is a cause for alarm. Consult your veterinarian.

FIRST AID

In general, a dog will heal his wounds by licking them. If he swallows anything harmful, chances are that he will throw it up. But it will probably make you feel better to help him if he is hurt, so treat his wounds as you would your own. Wash out the dirt and apply an antiseptic. If you are afraid that your dog has swallowed poison and you can't get to the veterinarian fast enough, try to induce vomiting by giving him a strong solution of salt water or mustard and water. Amateur diagnosis is dangerous, because the symptoms of so many dog diseases are alike. Too many people wait too long to take their dog to the doctor.

IMPORTANCE OF INOCULATIONS

With the proper series of inoculations, your dog will be almost completely protected against disease. However, it occasionally happens that the shot does not take, and sometimes a different form of the virus appears against which your dog may not be protected.

DISTEMPER

Probably the most virulent of all dog diseases is distemper. Young dogs are most susceptible to it, although it may affect dogs of all ages. The dog will lose his appetite, seem depressed, chilled, and run a fever. Often he will have a watery discharge from his eyes and nose. Unless treated promptly, the disease goes into advanced stages with infections of the lungs, intestines, and nervous system, and dogs that recover may be left with some impairment such as paralysis, convulsions, a twitch, or some other defect, usually spastic in nature. The best protection against this is very early inoculation with a series of permanent shots and a booster shot each year thereafter.

HEPATITIS

Veterinarians report an increase in the spread of this viral disease in recent years, usually with younger dogs as the victims. The initial symptoms — drowsiness, vomiting, great thirst, loss of appetite, and a high temperature — closely resemble those of distemper. These symptoms are often accompanied by swellings of the head, neck, and abdomen. The disease strikes quickly; death may occur in just a few hours. Protection is afforded by injection with a vaccine recently developed.

LEPTOSPIROSIS

This disease is caused by bacteria that live in stagnant or slow-moving water. It is carried by rats and dogs; infection is begun by the dog's licking substances contaminated by the urine or feces of infected animals. The symptoms are diarrhea and a yellowish-brown discoloration of the jaws, tongue, and teeth, caused by an inflammation of the kidneys. This disease can be cured if caught in time, but it is best to ward it off with a vaccine which your veterinarian can administer along with the distemper shots.

RABIES

This is an acute disease of the dog's central nervous system. It is spread by infectious saliva transmitted by the bite of an infected animal. Rabies is generally manifested in one of two classes of symptoms. The first is "furious rabies," in which the dog shows a period of melancholy or depression, then irritation, and finally paralysis. The first period lasts from a few hours to several days. During this time the dog is cross and will change his position often. He loses his appetite for food and begins to lick, bite, and swallow foreign objects. During the irritative phase the dog is spasmodically wild and has impulses to run away. He acts in a fearless manner and runs and bites at everything in sight. If he is caged or confined he will fight at the bars, often breaking teeth or fracturing his jaw. His bark becomes a peculiar howl. In the final, or paralytic, stage, the animal's lower jaw becomes paralyzed and hangs down; he walks with a stagger and saliva drips from his mouth. Within four to eight days after the onset of paralysis, the dog dies.

The second class of symptoms is referred to as "dumb rabies" and is characterized by the dog's walking in a bearlike manner, head down. The lower jaw is paralyzed and the dog is unable to bite. Outwardly it may seem as though he had a bone caught in his throat.

Even if your pet should be bitten by a rabid dog or other animal, he probably can be saved if you get him to the veterinarian in time for a series of injections. However, after the symptoms have appeared no cure is possible. But remember that an annual rabies inoculation is almost certain protection against rabies. If you suspect your dog of rabies, notify your local Health Department. A rabid dog is a danger to all who come near him.

COUGHS, COLDS, BRONCHITIS, PNEUMONIA

Respiratory diseases may affect the dog because he is forced to live under man-made conditions rather than in his natural environment. Being subjected to cold or a draft after a bath, sleeping near an air conditioner or in the path of a fan or near a radiator can cause respiratory ailments. The symptoms are similar to those in humans. The germs of these diseases, however, are different and do not affect both dogs and humans, so they cannot be infected by each other. Treatment is much the same as for a child with the same type of illness. Keep the dog warm, quiet, and well fed. Your veterinarian has antibiotics and other remedies to help the dog recover.

INTERNAL PARASITES

There are four common internal parasites that may infect your dog. These are roundworms, hookworms, whipworms, and tapeworms. The first three can be diagnosed by laboratory examination; the presence of tapeworms is determined by seeing segments in the stool or attached to the hair around the tail. Do not under any circumstances attempt to worm your dog without the advice of your veterinarian. After first determining what type of worm or worms are present, he will advise you of the best method of treatment.

EXTERNAL PARASITES

The dog that is groomed regularly and provided with clean sleeping quarters should not be troubled by fleas, ticks, or lice. If the dog should become infested with any of these parasites, he should be treated with a medicated dip bath or the new oral medications that are presently available.

SKIN AILMENTS

Any persistent scratching may indicate an irritation. Whenever you groom your dog, look for the reddish spots that may indicate eczema, mange, or fungal infection. Rather than treating your dog yourself, take him to the

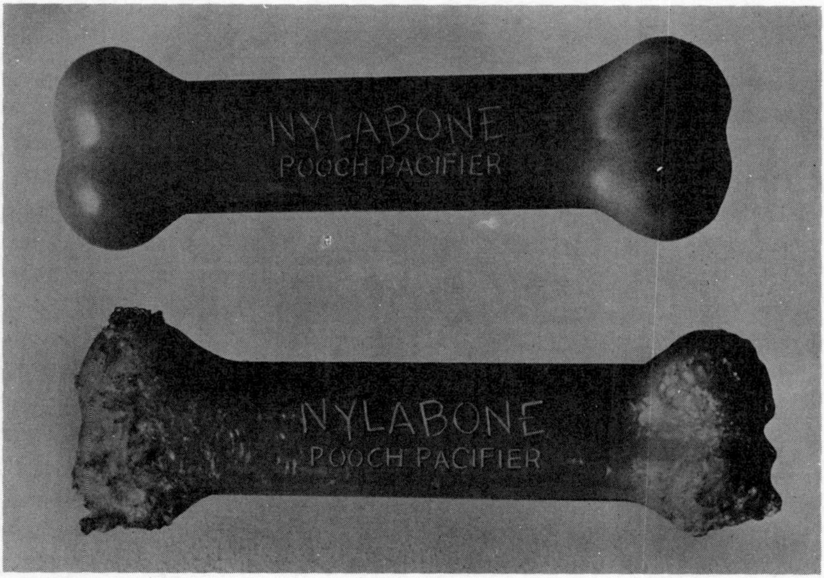

NYLABONE® is a necessity that is available at your local petshop (not in supermarkets). The puppy or grown dog chews the hambone flavored nylon into a frilly dog toothbrush, massaging his gums and cleaning his teeth as he plays. Veterinarians highly recommend this product . . . but beware of cheap imitations which might splinter or break.

veterinarian, as some of the conditions may be difficult to eradicate and can cause permanent damage to his coat.

EYES, EARS, TEETH, AND CLAWS

If you notice foreign matter collecting in the corners of your dog's eyes, wipe it out with a piece of cotton or tissue. If there is a discharge, check with your veterinarian.

Examine your dog's ears daily. Remove all visible wax, using a piece of cotton dipped in a boric acid solution or a solution of equal parts of water and hydrogen peroxide. Be gentle and don't probe into the ear, but just clean the parts you can see.

Don't give your dog bones to chew: they can choke him or puncture his intestines. Today veterinarians and dog experts recommend Nylabone, a synthetic bone manufactured by a secret process, that can't splinter or break even when pounded by a hammer. Nylabone will keep puppies from chewing furniture, aid in relieving the aching gums of a teething pup, and act as a toothbrush for the older dog, preventing the accumulation of tartar. Check your dog's mouth regularly and, as he gets older, have your veterinarian clean his teeth twice a year.

To clip your dog's claws, use specially designed clippers that are available at your petshop. Never take off too much of the claw, as you might

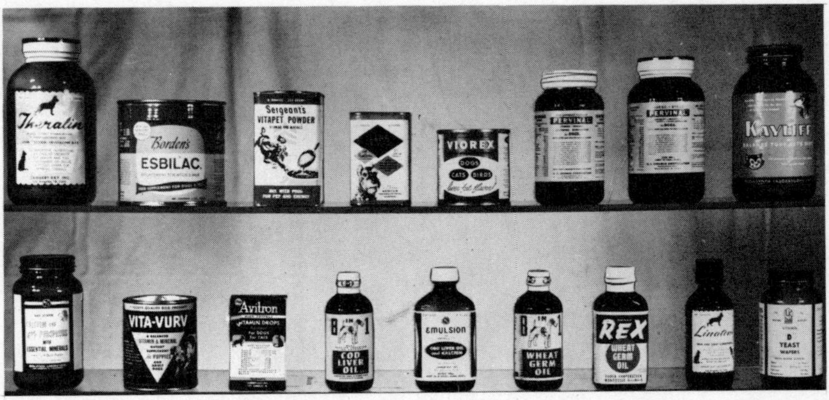

Active dogs and breeding bitches need food supplements. Visit your petshop for fresh vitamins and minerals to be added to your dog's diet.

cut the quick, which is sensitive and will bleed. Be particularly careful when you cut claws in which the quick is not visible. If you have any doubts about being able to cut your dog's claws, have your veterinarian or petshop do it periodically.

CARE OF THE AGED DOG

With the increased knowledge and care available, there is no reason why your dog should not live to a good old age. As the years go by he may need a little additional care. Remember that an excessively fat dog is not healthy, particularly as he grows older, so limit the older dog's food accordingly. He needs exercise as much as ever, although his heart cannot bear the strain of sudden and violent exertion. Failing eyesight or hearing means lessened awareness of dangers, so you must protect him more than ever.

Should you decide at this time to get a puppy, to avoid being without a dog when your old friend is no longer with you, be very careful how you introduce the puppy. He naturally will be playful and will expect the older dog to respond to his advances. Sometimes the old dog will get a new lease on life from a new puppy, but he may be consumed with jealousy. Do not give the newcomer the attention that formerly was exclusively the older dog's. Feed them apart, and show your old friend that you still love him the most; the puppy, not being accustomed to individual attention, will not mind sharing your love.

9. Showing

There is no greater pleasure for the owner than showing a beautiful dog perfectly groomed and trained for the show ring. Whether he wins or not, it is gratifying to show a dog in superb condition, one that is a credit to your training and care. A great deal of preparation, both for you and your dog, is needed before the day that you do any serious winning. Showing is not so easy as it looks, even if you have a magnificent dog. He must be presented to the judge so that all of his good points are shown to advantage. This requires practice in gaiting, daily grooming from puppyhood, and the proper diet to make him sound in body.

When you buy your puppy you probably will think he is the best in the country and possibly in the world, but before you enter the highly competitive world of dog shows, get some unbiased expert opinion. As your dog matures, compare him with the standard of his breed. Visit a few dog shows as a spectator and make mental notes of what is required of the handlers and dogs. Watch how the experienced handlers manage their dogs to bring out their best points.

TYPES OF DOG SHOWS

There are various types of dog shows. The American Kennel Club sanctioned matches are shows at which purebred dogs may compete, but not for championship points. These are excellent for you to enter to accustom you and your dog to showing. If your dog places in a few match shows, then you might seriously consider entering the big-time shows. An American Kennel Club all-breed show is one at which purebred dogs compete for championship points. An American Kennel Club specialty show is for one breed only. It may be held in conjunction with an all-breed show (by designating the classes at that show as its specialty show) or it may be held entirely apart. Obedience trials are different in that in them the dog is judged according to his obedience and ability to perform, not by his conformation to the breed standard.

There are two types of championship conformation shows: *benched* and *unbenched*. At a benched show your dog must be on his appointed bench during the advertised hours of the show's duration. He may be removed from the bench only to be taken to the exercise pen or to be groomed (an hour before showing) in an area designated for handlers to set up their crates and grooming tables. At an unbenched show your car may serve as a bench for your dog.

To become a champion your dog must win fifteen points in competition with other dogs; a portion of the fifteen points must be awarded as major point wins (three to five points) under different judges.

HOW TO ENTER

If your dog is purebred and registered with the AKC — or eligible for registration — you may enter him in the appropriate show class for which his age, sex, and previous show record qualify him. You will find coming shows listed in the different dog magazines or at your petshop. Write to the secretary of the show, asking for the premium list. When you receive the entry form, fill it in carefully and send it back with the required entry fee. Then, before the show, you should receive your exhibitor's pass, which will admit you and your dog to the show. Here are the five official show classes:

PUPPY CLASS: Open to dogs at least six months and not more than twelve months of age. Limited to dogs whelped in the United States and Canada.

NOVICE CLASS: Open to dogs six months of age or older that have never won a first prize in any class other than the puppy class, and less than three first prizes in the novice class itself. Limited to dogs whelped in the United States or Canada.

BRED BY EXHIBITOR CLASS: Open to all dogs, except champions, six months of age or over which are exhibited by the same person, or his immediate family, or kennel that was the recognized breeder on the records of the American Kennel Club.

AMERICAN-BRED CLASS: Open to dogs that are not champions, six months of age or over, whelped in the United States after a mating which took place in the United States.

OPEN CLASS: Open to dogs six months of age or over, with no exceptions.

In addition there are local classes, the Specials Only class, and brace and team entries.

For full information on dog shows, read the book *HOW TO SHOW YOUR OWN DOG,* by Virginia Tuck Nichols. (T.F.H.)

ADVANCED PREPARATION

Before you go to a show your dog should be trained to gait at a trot beside you, with head up and in a straight line. In the ring you will have to gait your dog around the edge with other dogs and then individually up and down the center runner. In addition the dog must stand for examination by the judge, who will look at him closely and feel his head and body structure. He should be taught to stand squarely, hind feet slightly back, head up on the alert. Showing requires practice training sessions in advance. Get a friend to act as judge and set the dog up and "show" him a few minutes every day.

Sometime before the show, give your dog a bath so he will look his best. Get together all the things you will need to take to the show. You will want to take a water dish and a bottle of water for your dog (so he won't be affected by a change in drinking water). Take your show lead, bench chain (if it is a benched show), combs and brush, and the identification ticket sent by the show superintendent, noting the time you must be there and the place where the show will be held, as well as the time of judging.

THE DAY OF THE SHOW

Don't feed your dog the morning of the show, or give him at most a light meal. He will be more comfortable in the car on the way, and will show more enthusiastically. When you arrive at the show grounds, find out where he is to be benched and settle him there. Your bench or stall number is on your identification ticket, and the breed name will be on placards fastened to the ends of the row of benches. Once you have your dog securely fastened to his stall by a bench chain (use a bench crate instead of a chain if you prefer), locate the ring where your dog will be judged (the number and time of showing will be on the program of judging which came with your ticket). After this you may want to take your dog to the exercise ring to relieve himself, and give him a small drink of water. Your dog will have been groomed before the show, but give him a final brushing just before going into the show ring. When your breed judging is called, it is your responsibility to be at the ringside ready to go in. The steward will give you an armband which has on it the number of your dog.

Then, as you step into the ring, try to keep your knees from knocking! Concentrate on your dog and before you realize it you'll be out again, perhaps back with the winners of each class for more judging and finally, with luck, it will be over and you'll have a ribbon and trophy — and, of course, the most wonderful dog in the world.

BIBLIOGRAPHY

PS-606 DOLLARS IN DOGS, by Leon F. Whitney, D.V.M. The 26 chapters of this beautifully useful book tell you—frankly and clearly—how you can make money in the dog field. Every avenue to profit through dogs is explored thoroughly by Dr. Whitney, famous veterinarian and breeder. There are no punches pulled in the discussions of money-making opportunities available to everyone who wants to profit through his connection with canines. A real career-builder, 254 pages of solid and practical information, illustrated.
ISBN #0-87666-290-4
8½ x 5½ 255 pages 60 black & white photos

PS-684 DOG HOROSCOPE—YOUR DOG NEEDS A BIRTHDAY. Probably the most clever and entertaining dog book ever published. Illustrated in color, readers are in for 64 pages of informative amusement, and you don't have to be an astrology fan to enjoy it.
ISBN #0-87666-317-X
8 x 5½ 64 pages 14 line illustrations

PS-607 HOW TO SHOW YOUR OWN DOG, by Virginia Tuck Nichols, paves the highroad to success in the fascinating and steadily growing avocation of exhibiting dogs. All of the intricacies of the show ring are explained in detail, coupled with wonderfully explicit treatments of the basics of dog shows; terms and definitions, how a champion is made, getting ready for the show, AKC rules and regulations, etc. Plus a bonus chapter on the tricks of the trade. In all, 254 well-illustrated pages that make winning in the dog show ring easier and a lot more fun.
ISBN #0-87666-390-0
8 ½ x 5½ 254 pages 136 black & white photos 10 line illustrations

H-925 DOG BREEDERS' HANDBOOK, by Ernest H. Hart. Here is the most complete and authoritative book on breeding ever written. In layman's language it clarifies all areas of this very necessary but often misunderstood subject. Beautifully presented and authored by a professional writer and recognized dog authority, the written word is augmented by profuse and pertinent illustrations.
ISBN #0-87666-286-6
85 black & white photos 12 line illustrations

PS-644 HOW TO TRAIN YOUR DOG, by Ernest H. Hart. Any dog is a better dog when well-trained. With the help of this book, any owner can do a first class job of training his dog. Fully and completely illustrated, the author takes you step by advancing step through the various areas of training. Many vital new concepts of training are advanced and discussed in this invaluable book. Color and black and white illustrations.
ISBN #0-87666-284-X
8½ x 5½ 107 pages 95 black & white photos 31 color photos

H-934 DOG OWNER'S ENCYCLOPEDIA OF VETERINARY MEDICINE, by Dr. Allan Hart. Here is a book that will become, next to his pet itself, the truest friend a dog-owner has. Page after page and chapter after chapter of valuable, pertinent information that allows an owner to make sure that his pet is given the best of care at all times. Easy to read yet brilliantly informative, this big book is a must.
ISBN #0-87666-287-4
8 x 5½ 186 pages 61 black & white photos 25 line illustrations